W99
(403)

MEDIEVAL WARFARE

MEDIEVAL WARFARE

AN ILLUSTRATED INTRODUCTION BY TIMOTHY NEWARK

BLOOMSBURY BOOKS LONDON

First published in 1979 by
JUPITER BOOKS (LONDON) LIMITED
167 Hermitage Road, London N4 1LZ.

Copyright © Timothy Newark 1979.

This edition published 1988 by
Bloomsbury Books an imprint of
Godfrey Cave Associates Limited
42 Bloomsbury Street, London WC1B 3QJ
under license from Minotaur Publishing Co Ltd
ISBN 1 870630 56 4

FOR MY FATHER

Printed in Yugoslavia

CONTENTS

AUTHOR'S NOTE

THE WARS and battles featured in this work are, in the main, those that took place in Britain and Western Europe – with particular attention given to the English and French.

The illustrations are all taken from my own collection; these are available from THE HISTORICAL PICTURE SERVICE, 86 Park Road, Brentwood, Essex CM14 4TT, England.

Timothy Newark

The Huns. The terrifying, centaur-like nomads who lived in the saddle, swept out of Asia into Europe, plundering and killing.

Chapter One

I

THE RISE OF THE HORSE-WARRIOR

N THE MILITARY context, the Middle Ages are best defined as the rise, supremacy, and decline of heavy cavalry as the principal force in battle. A significant development in warfare which spanned a period of more than a thousand years, from the fall of the Roman Empire in the fifth century A.D. to the decline of the armoured knight during the Renaissance of the fifteenth century.

This equestrian era began with a diffusion of vigorous martial horsemanship among the barbarian tribes living beyond the frontiers of the Roman Empire, a skill that originated in the immense plains of ancient Eurasia. The vast, treeless grasslands of the steppes could only be endured if travel was swift and far-reaching. The Asian nomads adopted the stocky, hardy horses indigenous to this region; thus horsemanship and horse culture developed and flourished. Indeed, one tribe believed itself descended from the coupling of a stallion and a woman.

This superb horse environment gave rise to several invaluable aids to riding, in particular the stirrup, a simple loop device attached to the saddle that gave greater stability and control to the horseman. Now secure on the animal's back, the rider could deliver a forceful charge with lance as well as a rapid, elusive attack with bow and arrow. With the incursion of these war-like, wandering tribes into Europe their horses combined with the heavier, larger mounts of the woodlands to produce an irresistible military power.

Up to this point in Europe, antiquity had featured the foot-soldier *en masse* as the principal force in battle. The horseman, by his greater mobility and economy had supplanted the charioteer, but still remained more or less a mounted foot-soldier subsidiary to the rest of the army. By the fourth century A.D. the Roman Empire, last stronghold of European antiquity, was on the verge of disintegration. Roman superiority in weapons and military morale was no longer so well defined. The barbarian tribes that penetrated every frontier were no longer half-naked savages, easy to subdue. Because of an ethnic upheaval in central Asia in which several mounted tribes, including the Huns, were forced to move west, Eastern ideas of warfare spread among the Germanic people.

Roman generals trained in traditional tactics were perplexed by the grow-ing numbers of horsemen the barbarians employed in battle: to remain in close order provided an easy target for horse-archers, while to extend and thin out formations made foot-soldiers vulnerable to a charge by lancers. The eclipse of Roman infantry supremacy by barbarian cavalry was most clearly illustrated in A.D. 378 in the battle of Adrianople (now Edirne in northern Turkey, near the border with Greece).

The Goths, originally from Scandinavia, had settled around the Black Sea and adopted the local horse culture. The migrations of the Huns forced the Goths to retreat within the Roman Empire. The Emperor Valens confronted the barbarian Goths with a Roman army near Adrianople, in Thrace.

The battle began with the Romans advancing on the enemy camp. The Goth cavalry were absent on a foraging expedition and the Goth infantry met the attack from behind barricades of wagons. In classical formation the Roman cohorts, supported on either flank by small squadrons of horse, pressed home the assault. Suddenly the Goth cavalry returned and fell upon the Roman left flank 'like a thunderbolt which strikes on a mountain top and dashes away all that stands in its path'. The Roman horsemen were routed and the infantry formations were compressed into a solid mass. In this chaotic conflict the inadequacy of the Roman short sword was demon-strated by the success of the lance and longer, heavier sword of the mounted Goths. Sir Charles Oman describes the scene:

'[The Romans] could not raise their arms to strike a blow, so closely were they packed. Spears snapped right and left, their bearers were unable to lift them into a vertical position; many soldiers were stifled in the press. Into this quivering mass the Goths rode, plying sword and lance against the helpless enemy. It was not till two-thirds of the Roman army had fallen that the thinning of the ranks enabled a few thousand men to break out and follow their right wing and cavalry in headlong flight.'

Adrianople was the worst defeat suffered by a Roman army since the disaster inflicted by Hannibal at Cannae in 216 B.C. After Adrianople the Roman armies underwent drastic changes in composition – both the numbers of cavalry and mercenaries were greatly increased. A trend well-reflected by the combined Roman-barbarian force that stopped the Huns at Chalons in A.D. 451. The Huns were the very embodiment of the savage horse-soldier, handling the Asiatic shortbow with remarkable dexterity, and invoking terrifying descriptions by their alien Mongol appearance:

'Nations whom they could never have defeated in fair fight fled in horror from those frightful faces, if indeed I may call them faces,' wrote a chronicler of the time, 'for they were nothing but shapeless black pieces of flesh, with little points instead of eyes. They have no hair on their cheeks or chins. Instead, the skin of their faces show deep furrowed scars; for hot irons are

Goth horse-warrior, the type that defeated the Roman army at Adrianople in A.D. 378 and established the supremacy of cavalry over infantry.

applied to the face of every boy that is born among them, so that blood is drawn before he is allowed to taste his mother's milk.'

Attila, the 'Scourge of God', had led his Huns throughout the eastern Roman Empire, now he turned towards the west and advanced into France. Near the town of Chalons the Huns were confronted by the half-Roman, half-German general Aetius with his army of Romans, Franks, Goths and other Teutonic tribes. The ensuing battle was fought by horse-archer and lancer against horse-archer and lancer. Aetius gained victory by sheer hard fighting, the manner of warfare for many centuries to come. Attila retreated back across the Rhine to ravage Italy.

With Rome itself captured in A.D. 410 by Alaric the Visigoth, the centre of Roman Imperialism was transferred to Constantinople in the east. Western Europe and the old Empire split up into various minor kingdoms ruled by Teutonic warlords. During the tribal migrations of the fourth and fifth centuries the Franks from north Germany settled new lands south of the Rhine. The Franks were significant in restoring some semblance of civiliz- ation to the chaos of post-Roman Europe. They were fortunate in having a

Frank leader Charles Martel defeating Moslem invaders at Tours in A.D. 732.

‡12‡

Frank horse-warrior at the
time of Charlemagne.

succession of dynamic leaders who established a united Frank Empire which
by the ninth century embraced France and parts of Germany, Spain, and
Italy making them the dominant power in western Europe.

It was within the Frank Empire that Feudalism and Knighthood evolved
to combat the anarchy constantly threatening its frontiers. With the development of the Frankish society and the cultivation of new land in Gaul, the
defence of its people could no longer have the totality of the armed tribe.
Therefore the responsibility of defence became the occupation of warriors
who devoted their lives to warfare. Thus the system of Feudalism, which is
basically the payment of land rent with service rather than with money,
became organized.

The king allocated land or estates to his lords who in return were duty
bound to contribute soldiers to a royal army in times of war. The major
landholders would subdivide their territories among lesser nobles for similar
service. If the kingdom lacked a strong ruler and centralized government,
this system would lead to local defence by individual lords. A lord obtained
the services of professional warriors by lending them a piece of land. This

‡13‡

Contemporary depiction of
Charlemagne (Charles the
Great) and his wife. Beneath,
his signature.

CHARLES THE GREAT AND HIS WIFE, AFTER THE EARLIEST PORTRAIT
(From the miniature of a MS. in the Library of the Monastery of St. Paul in Carinthia)
Beneath, the signature from a document of Charles' of the year 775

‡14‡

Act of homage between a knight and his lord, sealing the feudal contract. Seal of Raimond de Mont-Dragon.

enabled the warrior or knight to maintain his horses, armour, and weapons. The knight was now the vassal of his lord, as was the lord to his superior in the feudal hierachy.

The contract of Feudalism was usually sealed by an act of homage and an oath of fidelity; the piece of land on loan was called the 'fief'. The peasants who actually worked the land became the serfs of their warrior-tenants. In return for their labour the peasants received the protection of the knight. Within the system of Feudalism there was great oppression and exploitation. The peasants were subject to heavy taxes in order to support their knight, and were often levied into military service.

The impetus for the establishment of Feudalism in the Frank Empire in the early Middle Ages came especially from the incessant attacks of the Vikings in the north, the Avars and Magyars in the east, and the Moslems in the south. This also hastened the rise of effective cavalry among the Franks, who were originally foot-soldiers, as their enemies were all swift horsemen – even the maritime Vikings stole horses for their raids deeper inland. The development of Frank mailed cavalry consolidated Feudalism: the lords and knights introduced a code of conduct – chivalry – which clearly distinguished them from their land-working inferiors.

Thus we enter the age in which cavalry formed the strength of every feudal army, and the foot-soldiers – the serfs and peasantry – were esteemed as little in the camp as in the village. Such was the stratified class structure that when the strength of an opposing army was ascertained, only the knights were counted. The cult of chivalry fused Christian ideals with Germanic concepts of honour and loyalty, martial prowess was an essential part of this doctrine and from adolescence the practice of arms dominated the life of a knight (see Chapter Four, KNIGHTHOOD AND CHIVALRY).

The Frank Empire reached its zenith in the reign of Charlemagne (771–814), who extended his dominion from the Ebro to the Elbe. After his death, in the hands of weak successors his great empire fell to pieces. But the structure of Frank society left a powerful impression on western Europe and set the pattern of Feudalism and Knighthood that the energetic, horse-proud Normans adopted, perfected and brought to England. The horse-warrior was riding high and mighty.

Chapter Two

N

THE NORMAN CONQUESTS

ORMANS WERE the descendants of the Scandinavian Northmen who invaded France in the early tenth century. In order to contain these fierce, pagan warriors the French king, Charles the Simple, offered their leader, Rolf, a coastal province and his own daughter in marriage if he would turn Christian and stop harrying the country.

Rolf accepted the offer, embraced the Christian religion (and the French princess), was baptized in 912 under the name of Robert, and became the first Duke of Normandy (Northman's land) and a vassal of the French king. His followers likewise became Christians, abandoned their roving, piratical ways and established Normandy as one of the most powerful and progressive provinces of France.

Their descendants adopted the French language and culture but retained for a long time the marks of their Scandinavian origin and that warlike ardour that had made them so terrible in battle. Indeed, warfare and Christianity dominated their lives. They developed the art of horsemanship, delighted in hunting, gloried in sports and contests which fitted them for war, introduced improvement in weapons and armour, and for defence adopted the fortified wooden tower erected on a moated mound that evolved into the distinctive stone-built Norman keep and castle.

By the middle of the eleventh century, when Duke William ruled them, the energetic Normans were famed as the most active and enterprising people in Europe. Not only did they produce superb soldiers, but scholars among their clergy, able administrators, and skilled craftsmen and artists. Efficient in peace and war, these remarkable people spread their influence throughout Europe and the Middle East.

From 1020 onwards many Normans made their way through France to south Italy and offered their services to the highest bidder. Three sons of the Tancred family served the Greeks and were rewarded with grants of land. They soon repudiated their Greek paymasters and established themselves as independent princes. Their vigour and ruthless martial ability made them the admiration and terror of south Italy. In thirty years the brothers, supported by a few hundred other Normans, made themselves masters of southern Italy and before the end of the century had wrested Sicily from the Arabs. Other Norman leaders fought in Germany and Spain and won renown as crusaders in the Holy Land.

The greatest of all dukes of Normandy was William the Bastard, known to his contemporaries as William the Great, and called the Conqueror by historians long after his death. A warrior without equal in his lifetime, he became William I of England after defeating King Harold in the battle of Hastings in 1066, one of the hardest fought conflicts of the Middle Ages.

Born in 1027, William was the illegitimate son of Robert the Devil, Duke of Normandy, and Arletta, daughter of a tanner of Falaise. The great difference in their social positions prevented their marriage but Robert loved his bastard son and nominated him as his heir. When Robert died in 1035 while returning from a pilgrimage to Palestine, William found himself a child-ruler among the most turbulent baronage in Christendom. Treason and anarchy surrounded him as he grew to manhood. He matured into a most formidable adversary and positive ruler.

The very spirit of the Northmen seemed embodied in his gigantic form, his enormous strength, his savage countenance, his desperate bravery, the fury of his wrath, the ruthlessness of his revenge. 'No knight under heaven', his enemies confessed, 'was William's peer.' Malmesbury, an English chronicler of the twelfth century, tells us that William possessed 'such great strength of arm that none was able to draw his bow, which himself could bend when his horse was on full gallop'.

His anger was a terrible thing. When the rebelling people of Alençon

Northmen sailed up the Seine and attacked Paris in A.D. 845. To contain these wild raiders, Charles the Great simply offered them Normandy.

hung out raw hides along their walls and mocked the baseness of his birth (about which he was very sensitive) with cries of 'Work for the tanner!' he turned on his prisoners and had their eyes torn out, their hands and feet cut off, then flung them into the town.

William was an excellent field commander for his time. When Geoffry Martel, Count of Anjou invaded Normandy, William stayed his hand until the enemy column came to cross the river Dive. He allowed half the army to get over, then fell upon its rear. The battle raged till the rising tide cut the French force in two, as William had planned. Huddled together on a narrow causeway, swept by Norman arrows, knights, infantry and baggage train were all destroyed. Not a man escaped and Martel, who looked on helplessly from the opposite bank, fled home to die.

Having conquered Maine (the border land between Normandy and Angevin, which had been held by Anjou) and Brittany and married the daughter of the Count of Flanders, William looked further afield and settled his eyes on England. Here was the chance of gaining a throne which would give the Bastard equal status with the King of France. England was then ruled by the aging and childless Edward the Confessor, who thought highly of William and the Norman way of life.

After a difference with the Anglo-Saxon nobility, Edward saw fit to

Group of Normans in mail hauberks. Note characteristic kite-shaped shield and helmet with nasal.

recognize William as his heir. To further his claim to the English throne, the devious duke exacted a promise of support from his most likely rival to the crown, Harold Godwine, Earl of Wessex. Apparently the promise was forced from Harold when he was shipwrecked in 1062 off the Normandy coast and fell into William's grasping hands. To gain his freedom he made an oath of allegiance to the Norman, which he later repudiated as being made under duress.

When Edward died in January 1066 Harold, who during the last years of Edward's feeble rule was virtual administrator of the Anglo-Saxon realm, was elected king by the Witan, the assembly of wise men. On hearing the news of Harold's accession, William was speechless with rage. Deprived of what he considered to be his rightful inheritance, the angry duke determined to take the crown by force.

William's fame as a victorious warrior attracted knights to his banner from all over Normandy and France, on the understanding that if they defeated Harold they would be rewarded with large estates in conquered England. The exact size of William's invasion army is unknown. Various historians have estimated its strength from 7,000 to 60,000. Sir Charles Oman suggests a figure of 32,000 of which 12,000 were cavalry. A large portion of the infantry were archers, some armed with the shortbow (which was pulled back to the chest), and the mechanical crossbow.

The Norman knight of this period wore a chain mail tunic down to his knees, split fore and aft to the crutch to enable him to ride comfortably. Some tunics had chain mail leggings, most had mail hoods to cover the throat and head (leaving the face bare), over which was worn a conical

Normans carrying arms and provisions for the invading fleet. From the Bayeux Tapestry.

‡21‡

The Norman invasion force lands at Pevensey, Sussex, in 1066.

helmet with a 'nasal', or nose guard. He carried a sword and lance, the latter wielded javelin fashion, not couched under the arm in the manner of the knight of later years. The shield he carried was long and kite-shaped to give him adequate protection in the saddle.

Harold not only had William's hostility to contend with but also that of his outlawed brother Tostig, who had taken refuge in Norway and secured the aid of its king, Harald Hardrada. When Tostig and the Norwegian king landed on the coast of Yorkshire on 18 September 1066, Harold marched September he met and defeated the enemy at Stamford Bridge. Both Tostig and Hardrada were killed in the battle.

Three days later William landed at Pevensey in Sussex. Augustin Thierry (*The Norman Conquest of England*) describes the invasion force:

'The archers landed first; they wore short habits, and had their hair shaven off. The cavaliers landed next, clad in coats of mail and wearing helmets of polished iron, nearly of a conical shape; armed also with long heavy lances and with straight two-edged swords. After them came the workmen of the army, pioneers, carpenters and smiths, who unloaded on the shore, piece by piece, three wooden castles, framed and prepared beforehand.'

William proceeded to lay waste the south coast in order to hastily bring Harold to battle. Although Harold marched with all speed from York to Hastings, he refused to attack the Norman invaders on ground of William's choosing. He advanced near enough to the coast to check William's ravages and entrenched himself on a hill, known afterwards as that of Senlac, a low spur of the Sussex Downs some eight miles north-west of Hastings.

Harold organized his army for a defensive stand and his position on the

William the Bastard reviews
his troops on the Sussex shore.
Knights from all over France
had joined his standard.

Anglo-Saxon warrior as depicted in an old MS.

Saxon spearman with typical round shield and defensive armour of animal hide. Also shown, a hand-flail of bronze.

ridge, athwart the road to London, was strengthened by a stockade of stakes; his flanks were anchored in marshy, broken ground. His force has been estimated as numbering 20,000, with a frontage so densely packed, about twenty men deep, that their bristling spear shafts looked like a forest.

The 'housecarls' (royal guard) formed the centre of the Anglo-Saxon line at the highest point; here stood Harold with his brothers Gyrth and Leofwine between the Golden Dragon banner of Wessex and the royal standard, the Fighting Man. The housecarls were superb, disciplined, professional warriors clad in chain mail of the Norman style, armed with a long battle axe, a single-bladed head of great size fitted to a shaft five feet in length. Both hands and a lot of muscle were required to wield this fearsome weapon which neither shield nor mail could resist; a single stroke could chop off a horse's head.

The housecarls were the nucleus of a makeshift army mainly composed of the 'fyrd', or local peasant militia, levied for the occasion. The fyrd were undisciplined, destitute of armour, and carried a motley array of weapons, spears, swords, clubs and even slings for hurling stones. The typical Anglo-Saxon shield was circular with a prominent boss in the centre. All of Harold's army were on foot and he had few, if any, archers.

Eager to begin the battle, William marched towards Harold's strong position and opened the contest soon after dawn on 14 October. Just before he ordered his troops to advance, he addressed them:

'Remember to fight well and put all to death. For if we conquer we shall

all be rich. What I gain, you will gain; if I conquer, you will conquer. If I take this land, you shall have it. Know, however, that I am not come here only to obtain my right, but also to avenge our whole nation for the felonies, perjuries, and treacheries of these English . . . Come then, and let us, with God's help, chastise them for all their misdeeds.'

The Normans advanced in three lines: the archers in front, followed by the infantry, and in the rear the mounted knights. The plan of attack was simple enough. The archers were to thin out and weaken the enemy ranks with a storm of arrows and bolts, then the infantry would assault and breach the position, thus providing a gap through which the Norman horse could charge.

Attacking uphill is a handicap from the start. The arrows of the Norman archers were either deflected by the wall of Saxon shields or flew harmlessly overhead. When the infantry dashed up the slope they met with an avalanche of spears and stones; the Normans who managed to reach the enemy were chopped down by sword and axe to the furious Saxon cry 'Out! Out!'

With his foot-soldiers thrown back in some disorder, William launched his horsemen up the hill but they too were repulsed. In this initial cavalry charge, Thierry tells us that:

Bishop Odo, half-brother of William, carrying a baton of command, encourages the Normans in the battle of Hastings. From the Bayeux Tapestry.

'A Norman knight named Taillefer spurred his horse forward in front and began the song of the exploits of Charlemagne and Roland. As he sang he played with his sword, throwing it with force in the air, and receiving it again in his right hand. The Normans joined in chorus, or cried, "God be our help! God be our help!"'

Alone, Taillefer rushed straight at the shield wall and struck down several of the enemy before an axe blow finished him. In his brief moment of glory, Taillefer the minstrel-warrior embodied both the berserker battle madness of his Viking forefathers and the romantic spirit of knightly chivalry.

Again and again William rallied his battered men and led them up the body-strewn slope, but they could not penetrate the stout Saxon line. The duke had several horses killed under him and his soldiers, on hearing that he was dead, fled down the hill in a growing panic. Some of Harold's undisciplined and inexperienced peasant levies, encouraged by the sight of the enemy departing in such fear and haste, left their position to go in pursuit.

This appears to have been a crucial moment of the battle. The Normans were confused and demoralized. They believed their leader to be dead. If Harold had ordered a general advance at this stage he might have won the day decisively. But he stood firm in the security of his static position. William dealt with his shaky situation by riding among his fleeing men, cursing and striking them with a lance. Removing his helmet so that his disheartened soldiers could recognize him, he shouted: 'Here I am. Look at me. I live and with God's help I will conquer yet!'

Rallying his troops, William turned upon the Saxon pursuers and cut the amateur warriors to pieces. In leading another charge the implacable duke

Duke William, left, directing his knights in the fight at Hastings. The Normans used their lances for thrusting and throwing. From the Bayeux Tapestry.

rode straight at the royal standard. Unhorsed yet again, the terrible William struck dead Harold's brother Gyrth with his bone-crushing mace and then pulled a Norman from the saddle to gain a mount. Leofwine fell to the sword of Roger de Montgomerie.

But still the Saxon wall stood unbroken and the Normans were forced to withdraw. William now decided to lure more of Harold's impetuous levies into pursuit in order to destroy them piecemeal. He commanded his men to feign flight and panic. Several times the deception worked and large numbers of peasants were slaughtered at the base of the hill. The veteran housecarls, however, stood tight-packed and firmly rooted on the crest, unmoved by every Norman dash and device.

William ordered his archers to the front, instructing them to shoot high in the air so that their arrows fell 'like bolts from heaven' on the massed housecarls, who suffered greatly under the raining missiles. Harold himself was struck in the eye by an arrow but continued to fight on. Now the battle swung in full favour of the Normans. The cavalry plunged through the Saxon ranks, scattering the enemy and exploiting the horseman's high advantage over the foot-soldier. Under the flailing hooves and blades the surviving fyrd fell apart and melted away. Only the valiant housecarls remained fighting to the last man around their blood-drenched, wounded king, who was slain by four Norman knights who 'killed him with many blows, sorely mangling his body'.

By nightfall the battle was over and William made his camp on the field of gore to eat and drink among the dead. He had won a kingdom and was crowned in London on Christmas Day 1066. The Norman Conquest revolutionized English society and changed the course of history. William introduced a total alteration of the state of English law and property by dividing all the lands into baronies and adopting the feudal constitution of Normandy in regard to tenure and services.

The battle of Hastings, or Senlac, was one of the hardest fought conflicts of the Middle Ages, a desperate struggle in which William's tactics and his combined use of cavalry and archers eventually triumphed over the stiff resistance of the Anglo-Saxon foot-soldiers. Military historians have made much significance of the Norman horsemen being the decisive factor in the fight, as if victory was inevitable to the commander with cavalry. But Hastings was a close run thing indeed. With more housecarls and better disciplined auxiliaries, Harold would have triumphed; the Normans would have dashed themselves into defeat against the Saxon rock.

King Harold was struck in the eye by an arrow at the height of the battle of Hastings and was later hacked to death. Note the housecarl in the foreground cleaving a Norman's skull with his axe.

Nevertheless, William's great victory established a military pattern that lasted for three centuries: not even the finest infantry, armed for close combat, could overcome armoured horsemen in the open. The cavalry cult had arrived in England and her mailed and mounted knights born of Anglo-Saxon-Norman blood would dominate the fields of many battles to come.

Chapter Three   ARMS AND ARMOUR

ROM THE barbarians of the early Middle Ages to the worthy crusader knights of the high Middle Ages the principal body armour was a coat of mail, generally referred to as the 'hauberk'. Weapons changed little from ancient times – the sword, spear, and axe remained the basic arms of war. This was the age of ascendancy of the armoured horseman: the mail-clad knight being the dominant force in warfare. The turning point, however, came in the fourteenth century with the advent of gunpowder and the resurgence of the foot-soldier. Polearms and the longbow in the hands of organized infantry gave them a decisive influence in battle not witnessed since the time of the Roman legionary. And in particular the development of gunpowder weapons generated the adoption of full plate armour by the knights of the late Middle Ages.

During the early period of the Middle Ages the characteristic arms of the barbarian Scandinavian and German tribes were the battle axe and the round wooden shield. The huge Viking axe, with a haft five feet in length, was wielded by both hands. A formidable weapon indeed, it was capable of cutting down horse and man at a single blow. It was used with great effect by King Harold's housecarls against the Normans at Hastings in 1066. The

Vikings on a plundering
expedition. These fierce sea-
rovers favoured the battle-axe
and round wooden shield,
covered with leather and
strengthened with metal.

axe used by the Franks was called a 'francisca', a broad-edged blade with a short haft, often employed as a missile; the Franks were skilled in throwing it and seldom missed their target.

The shield typical of the time was round in shape, about three feet in diameter, made of wood reinforced with strips of iron or bronze, its metal rim and prominent boss making it useful in attack as well as defence. The sword of the period was a double-edged, heavy slashing weapon, a suitable representation of an era noted for its crude and crushing warfare. The sword among the Franks was only a horseman's weapon, a traditional concept continued for several centuries, the sword becoming the symbolic arm of the knight. The bow and arrow in this early period, although used with terrific effect by Asian horsemen, was regarded in western Europe as a secondary weapon more suited to hunting.

The majority of warriors at this time wore their everyday clothes in battle, perhaps strengthened with leather and strips of metal or quilted cloth, but relying mainly on the shield for protection. Effective body armour in the form of chain mail being an expensive commodity. The Vikings enjoyed a distinct advantage in battle because their extensive plundering enabled

French knight of 12th century wearing mail hauberk with coif, or mail hood, under dome-shaped helmet with nasal.

them to obtain more mail armour than their contemporaries. The Vikings favoured a short mail shirt called a *brynija*.

The hauberk, or long mail coat, was popular with the knights of Charlemagne's Frank Empire; it was split in the front and back to facilitate riding. Mail armour was made in other forms than that of interlocking iron rings. The latticed hauberk was fashioned out of several layers of material with wadding between each, then quilted and kept together by strips of leather placed to form diamond-shaped spaces, a ring or nail-head then being sewn in each space and also on every interlocking angle. Coats of scale armour, composed of overlapping lozenge-shaped pieces of metal, were also worn.

The Viking settlement in Frankish Normandy fused two significant military cultures: the resulting Norman race produced a magnificent crop of conquering, mail-clad heavy horsemen. The kite-shaped Norman shield was designed for mounted fighting, giving a knight protection from shoulder to foot; when not in use the shield was carried slung over the back. The Norman spear was a combination lance and javelin, used by the knights for thrusting and throwing. The Norman-style hauberk had a 'coif', or mail hood, which left only the face exposed; over the coif was worn the distinctive conical helmet fitted with a 'nasal', an iron extension to protect the nose.

By the thirteenth century the knight of the high Middle Ages was enveloped in mail armour: both the arms and the legs were covered, even the hands were protected by mittens of mail. Under the hauberk the knight

Early 13th century knight in complete suit of mail armour, with face-enveloping helm, small shield and surcoat. His horse is covered with a cloth caparison adorned with heraldic emblems. Seal of Robert Fitz-Walter.

wore a padded coat of leather or felt called a 'gambeson'. The helmet nasal had fallen from favour because it provided a useful grip for an enemy in close combat; King Stephen was captured in this manner at Lincoln in 1141. The small, close-fitting helmet was superseded by the massive 'helm', a barrel-shaped helmet pierced with slits and holes for vision and for breathing. This ponderous helm was carried suspended by a small chain from the saddle day and night along the Roman road from London to York and on 25 and was assumed by the knight only when going into action.

The flat-topped helm later gave way to one of conical shape, which provided a glancing surface for the blows of sword or mace. However, this helmet design caused such blows to be deflected downwards on the shoulders; to combat this, curious-looking little plates called 'ailettes' were attached to the shoulders, sloping towards the helmet. The lower limbs, always vulnerable to foot-soldiers, were also given plate protection in the form of 'greaves' for the shins and 'poleyns' for the knees.

The increase of body armour lessened the necessity of a shield, which decreased in size and shape to that of the traditional heraldic shield. The growing totality of armour and the face-enveloping helm made it virtually impossible to identify a knight in battle. Thus evolved the art and science of heraldry. The linen 'surcoat', adopted by the crusaders from the Saracens, proved an ideal garment for sporting a knight's family emblem. The armoured knight had perhaps reached the zenith of his power on the battlefield. At Bouvines in 1214 it is said that the knightly armour was in such

French man-at-arms, early
13th century, wearing mail
from head to toe and what
appear to be metal greaves
over the front of his legs.

perfect condition, the mail so closely worked, that the only way to kill an unhorsed knight was to beat him to death.

The sword developed in accordance with the increase in body armour; long, narrow blades, stiffened through a diamond-shaped cross section, were designed to pierce rather than cut through mail. The 'falchion', a wide, curved, single-edged sword of Eastern origin, was introduced. The grip of the sword was lengthened to give greater balance and striking power. Pommels were made larger to counter the weight of the blades. The sword was no longer the apanage of the knight and was used by all soldiers. In addition to his sword, a knight carried a short, triangular stabbing dagger to exploit any vital joints in the armour of an unhorsed enemy.

Throughout the early and high Middle Ages the common foot-soldier was a much scorned, ill-armed pawn, often ridden down by his own knights

Great helm of the 14th century. This type of heavy helmet was only put on at the moment of going into action.

impatient to close with the enemy. The French chivalry, in particular, were noted for their utter contempt of the humble infantry, whereas the English knights, perforce, came to respect their foot-soldiers, especially the trained longbowmen of the Hundred Years War. Consisting usually of local peasants hurriedly levied, foot-soldiers fought with the weapon nearest to hand – agricultural tools such as flails, sickles, hayforks, and great fencing hammers. They were generally regarded as worthless rabble to be sacrificed in the opening stages of battle.

But times were changing. The imperious role of the mounted warrior came to a crisis with the surprising victories of two particular pedestrian forces in the fourteenth century. At Crécy (1346) and Poitiers (1356) during the Hundred Years War, English longbowmen devastated the finest of French Knighthood. In the battles of Mortgarten (1315) and Sempach (1386) in Switzerland, Swiss foot-soldiers armed with the long pike defeated the large feudal armies of their Hapsburg overlords. The reason for these successes lay in tactical order and homogenity of weapons. The English yeomen fought with the powerful, long-range bow and arrow in prepared

positions, supported by a steel nucleus of dismounted men-at-arms. The Swiss mountainmen, armed with formidable pikes, twenty-one feet long, advanced in a deep, close formation similar to the phalanx of the ancient Greeks.

Initially, out of poor circumstance, even the best of foot-soldiers were lightly armoured. The extent of infantry protection being usually a quilted leather jacket, an iron skull-cap, and a little round shield called a 'buckler'. However, this light attire often worked to their advantage by giving them greater agility in close combat and speed in manoeuvre. Veteran foot-soldiers acquired mail hauberks, pieces of plate armour, and helmets taken from dead or captured knights on the battlefield, or by being employed as professional soldiers in mercenary armies. And the crude farming implements of earlier times developed into the family of polearms which included the 'halberd', the 'partisan', the 'bill', the 'poleaxe', and the 'guisarme'; weapons which generally combined a broad cutting edge with a piercing spike, or a crushing hammer, or a hook for unhorsing a knight. All were fixed on long shafts.

Instrumental in this curtailment of the established power of the heavy horseman was the invention of gunpowder weapons. Before the wide application of gunpowder in warfare, a combustible composition called 'Greek fire' was much employed. Of ancient origin, this flaming, frightening substance which included naptha, sulphur, and pitches (its exact mixture is unknown) was either ejected through pipes, by means of a bellows, to set fire to shipping or military engines, or flung in containers by giant catapults. It was also used in crude hand grenades in close combat. The terror of Greek fire was compounded by the fact that it could not be extinguished by water, only urine, vinegar or sand could put it out.

The composition of gunpowder is claimed to have been introduced to Europe by the circulation of Arabic scientific literature. In 1242 the monk Roger Bacon recorded its ingredients as: 'But of saltpetre take 7 parts, 5 of young hazle-twigs [charcoal], and 5 of sulphur; and so thou wilt call up thunder and destruction, if thou know the art.' The invention of gunpowder ruined Feudalism, for firearms proved to be the great leveller in warfare.

One of the first known uses of cannon in open battle is generally accepted to have been at Crécy in 1346; several 'bombards' as they were called, were

French knight of the late 13th century wearing flat-topped helm.

English knight of the late 13th century showing the mode in which the coif was fastened at the side of the head. His mail mittens have metal-free palms to give a firmer grasp. His lance bears the knightly pennon and the figure at the top right holds his great helm.

‡40‡

Knight of the end of the 13th century in mail armour with additional plate protection on the knees and elbows. He wears a conical helm with a visor. Note the way his saddle curves about his waist, holding him secure.

placed between the companies of English bowmen and 'with fire threw little iron balls to frighten the French horses'. At the siege of Calais in 1347 the English built a castle of wood and armed it with bombards. In the beginning of the fifteenth century nearly all the countries of Europe were provided with cannons. An old writer describes these guns as 'vomiting from their fiery mouths vast quantities of stones, with a vehement explosion and a terrific and intolerable noise'.

The earliest guns took the form of small metal jugs or tubes set on the ground, hence their names *pot-de-fer*, *vasa*, and cannon (from the Latin *canna* for reed). They were ignited either with a red-hot rod poked through a hole in the breach or by a lighted match or fuse. At first these crude cannons were useful as noise-makers; they proved no rival in range or effect to the longbow and crossbow. However, interest in the construction of guns continued and by the fifteenth century there was a wide range of artillery.

Huge bombards were built and by sheer weight of shot succeeded in blasting down the walls of previously impregnable castles. In size, the cannon was taken to extremes in such monsters as the Scottish 'Mons Meg', thirteen feet long, which could fire a nineteen-and-a-half inch iron ball over a distance of a mile. Even bigger was a Turkish siege gun that weighed

The battle of Bouvines, in Northern France, 1214, in which it was said that knightly armour was so perfect, that the only way to kill an unhorsed knight was to beat him to death.

nineteen tons; the Russian 'King of Cannons' had a barrel seventeen feet long and discharged a one-ton stone ball. The great bombards were virtually immobile and very slow to load. They were mounted on earthworks and were useful only in sieges.

In the fifteenth century wrought-iron cannons bound in the manner of wooden barrels were superceded by cannon cast in iron or brass and mounted on wheeled carriages of a rough type. Lighter, mobile guns could now be employed in the battlefield. The first 'hand cannons' date from the late fourteenth century and took the form of a narrow iron tube, about two to three feet long, mounted on a pike staff and held under the armpit, where it could be fired in the general direction of the enemy. These primitive hand-guns were thoroughly unreliable, often causing injury to their operatives.

The renaissance of the foot-soldier and the advent of guns hastened the trend towards full plate armour in the fourteenth century. A plate of steel had been worn underneath the hauberk to protect the knight's chest; this now became the externally worn breastplate. The hauberk was shortened and additional pieces of plate armour developed into leg and arm guards. The great helm was still popular but now had a moveable face piece, or

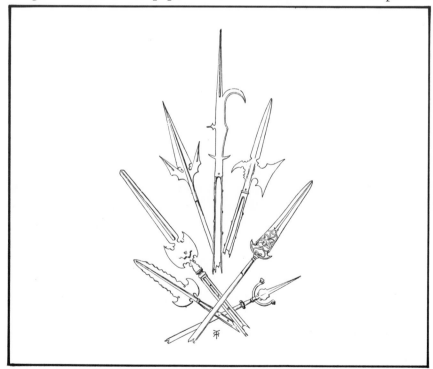

The family of polearms, various shaped heads for thrusting, hacking, and hooking horsemen out of the saddle, all fixed to long shafts.

Group depicting arquebus, longbow, polearms, cannon, and two men in the centre about to hurl grenades of 'Greek fire', a primitive kind of napalm.

'visor'. Under the helm a smaller helmet, or 'bascinet', was worn. The coif was superseded by the 'aventail', a sheet of mail separate from the hauberk, that was attached to the bascinet and hung down over the shoulders.

During this period many knights, especially the English, suppressed their pedestrian prejudice, accepted the vulnerability of horsemen faced with the longbow and pike, and began to fight on foot. The long surcoat was shortened to the tight-fitting 'gipon'.

The transition from mail to plate was complete by the beginning of the fifteenth century. The knight of the late Middle Ages was now totally encased in a suit of plate armour. What had begun as a collection of separate plates had become a system of articulated steel. Mail could only be seen as filling the joints between plates. Gauntlets were made of several thin segments of steel enabling the hand to move freely. There was armour for the feet, with long pointed toes reflecting the fashionable dress of the time. The massive helm, like the shield, had been relegated to the tournament, while the bascinet and aventail were succeeded by the great visored bascinet with both neck and throat guards incorporated.

‡44‡

Suits of armour were now constructed with immense skill and beauty by master craftsmen and, apparently in acknowledgment of this, knights no longer wore the covering gipon over their magnificent armour. The most desirable suits of armour were those made by the armourers of northern Italy and their keenest rivals in southern Germany; these two schools of armour developed distinctive styles.

Italian armour, produced principally in Milan, was notable for its large and simple curves of plate. Metal ribs were hammered up across the surface to direct sword blows from vital areas. As in jousting armour, the left shoulder plates were enlarged to cover and reinforce the 'target' side of the knight. A lance rest was attached to the right breast. A series of hoops extended over the hips and to these were fixed 'tassets' to protect the thighs. A new close helmet, or 'armet', replaced the bascinet with its restrictive neck guards.

German, or Gothic armour was remarkable for its heavily fluted and pointed appearance, a result of the greater number of plates used in its composition. The fluting gave the armour increased strength without extra weight, as well as providing a glancing face to weapons. The helmet characteristic of Gothic armour was the 'sallet', with its sweeping neck guard. Where the two styles of armour mixed, as with the armourers of Flanders, a combination of fluting with tassets and reinforced shoulders was produced.

By the end of the fifteenth century plate armour had attained its highest

Robert the Bruce, King of Scotland, kills the English knight Sir Humphrey Bohun with a single blow of his battle-axe, at the opening of the battle of Bannockburn in 1314.

development, even the horse of the period was protected by plates everywhere except on the legs, often having a unicorn spike attached to the head armour, the 'chanfron'. It has been estimated that a knight's suit of armour plus mail shirt weighted about seventy pounds. It is a popular misconception that an unhorsed knight, felled to the ground, was reduced to the helpless status of a tortoise on his back. This is not true. Because his suit of steel was so well articulated and evenly distributed over his body, the fully armoured knight was quite mobile and could easily mount his horse without any form of aid. The suggestion that he was lowered into the saddle by a kind of crane device is nonsense. The chief problem of fighting in a full suit of armour was that of insufficient ventilation. Many knights were suffocated in the press of battle.

The principal weapons of the knight in this period remained fundamentally as before – the lance, sword, battle-axe, and mace – the only difference being one of massiveness as might be expected from the resistance they had to meet. The mace, having evolved from a simple wooden club,

German knight wearing Gothic armour, an illustration based on the engraving 'The Knight, Death and the Devil' by Albrecht Dürer (1513). Note the sallet, the helmet with sweeping neckguard characteristic of Gothic armour.

‡47‡

Armour of the middle of the
15th century, a mixture of the
Italian and Gothic styles,
probably made in Flanders.

do untredeu tu de boden des soldanes · De keiser uor do uord
to konin de heidenen studden mit ene unde worden sege
los bi der star. ete ward uminace uile geslagen · Sin sone
de herroge vrederic gewan dewile destar unde herbergede
dar in. En burch lach binnen der star dar was de soldan
uppe · vor der burch lagen de xpenen alsd lange wanne se den
soldan dar to dwungen dar he in des gule gaf dar se had
den guden vrede unde guden kop al dur sin lant · Do de
keiser dannen vor de heidenen braken den vrede des behelt
de keiser de gisle unde uorde se mit eme to armenie dar

Fredericus

wolde de keiser swemmen men
unde vordrank · Do ward grot
iamer in der xpenheit · Do starf
oc greue ludolf unde greue
wilbranc van halremunt unde der xpenen uele des kei
seres begrouen en del to anthioc dar ander del uordrenen
to surs unde begrof ir dar mid groten eren · De herroge unde

The death, by drowning, of Frederick Barbarossa, Holy
Roman Emperor, during the Third Crusade. From the
Gotha MS of the Saxon Chronicle written in the second half
of the 13th century.

A fine example of late 15th-century horse armour with crinet, or neck protection, and chanfron, or face guard with unicorn spike.

became a favourite knightly bone-crusher. The *Morgenstern* ('morning-star') was much favoured by the German and Swiss; in its basic form it comprised a wooden ball studded with iron spikes on a long shaft. It is said that the star-shaped mace 'received its name from the ominous jest of wishing the enemy good-morning with the morning-star when they had been surprised in camp or city'.

The military 'flail', composed of a shaft to which chains and spiked iron balls were attached, was dubbed the 'holy-water sprinkler' from its shape and from the blood which spurted from its victims; the flail was often mounted on long shafts to join the family of polearms. The huge two-handed sword became popular with foot-soldiers, especially among the German *Landsknechts* and the Swiss, the latter using the 'flamberg' with its flame-shaped blade.

The great advance in weaponry during the fifteenth century came in the field of firearms. A wooden stock was fitted to the barrel of the hand-cannon which enabled the gun to be held against the shoulder and resulted in more accurate shooting. From the curved, hooked shape of the stock these early firearms gained their names of 'hackbus' and 'arquebus'. The 'matchlock' was a significant invention in the evolution of firearms. Previously, the firing mechanism of a gun had consisted of a pan filled with priming powder connected to the powder charge inside the barrel via a touch-hole; all this had been located on the top of the breech and had subsequently greatly inconvenienced aiming and firing.

With the matchlock, the pan and touch-hole were moved to the side of the gun, also being protected from the weather by a 'lockplate'. The slow-burning cord match which set off the priming powder was then held in an S-shaped mechanism, called the 'serpentine', and attached to the side of the gun by means of a pivot. The actual 'lock' consisted of levers joining the serpentine to a trigger. By the start of the sixteenth century the matchlock arquebus was in wide use throughout Europe.

The gun was beginning to shape history. French artillery defeated the

Swiss soldiers of the 15th century wearing Gothic-inspired armour and armed with polearms and hand-cannon.

Arquebusier of the 16th century. Note the 'serpentine' device on the matchlock and the ammunition pouch at his right side.

English at Formigny and Castillon and ended the Hundred Years War. In 1453 the Ottoman Turks captured the Byzantine Christian bastion of Constantinople with a siege train of seventy heavy cannon. Speed of manoeuvre was now a more effective defence than thickness of armour. Paradoxically, it was during this period that some of the finest plate armour seen in Europe was produced. Most suits of armour of the sixteenth century were made solely for parade and state occasions; they were status symbols and imitated the current fashions, a splendid example being the armour made for Emperor Charles V in the Roman–Graeco style. In battle, armour was usually reduced to a breastplate and open helmet. The role of the knight in warfare was coming to an end. A lifetime's experience in handling weapons was no longer essential, a simple gun was sufficient and much less expensive. The professional infantryman armed with pike or arquebus had become the principal power in battle.

A knight and his squire.

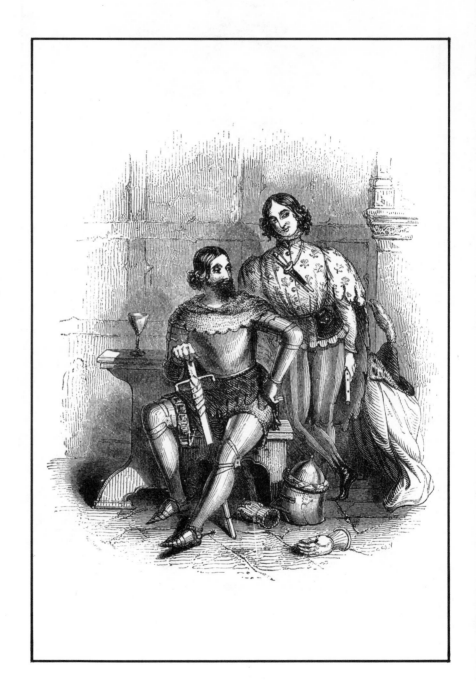

Chapter Four

KNIGHTHOOD AND CHIVALRY

ARMOURED KNIGHTS, mounted high on heavy horses, were the most esteemed warriors of the feudal army. A proud, professional fighting man raised from youth in the martial skills and imbued with the high ideals of chivalry, the knight represented the mailed fist of his lord and monarch. When the war drums beat he was the first to join the royal standard, providing his own armour and mounts. In times of peace he exercised his skill at arms in fierce tournaments and friendly jousts with his peers.

Fighting was his trade and chivalry his creed, the latter being the codified system of Knighthood. The true knight was supposed to be pious, truthful, a gallant warrior, magnanimous in victory, a generous friend, and a devoted lover. To this could be added a gentleness of manners and culture of mind. It was his chivalric duty to wield the sword of justice, to strike down the tyrant, to protect womanhood, help the weak and innocent, and give his life, if need be, in the causes of his church and monarch. But all too often, alas, knights were false to those splendid ideals, especially when dealing with the lower orders who were not covered, apparently, by the cloak of chivalry.

It is difficult to fix a certain date when chivalry first took root. According

to Tacitus, the Roman historian (*c*.54–120), customs bearing a resemblance
to those of chivalry existed in his day among the German nations. On the
fall of Rome these Teutonic tribes subdued and colonized the country now
called France and it is probable that they planted the germ of chivalry. The
first traces of its existence in France appeared in the days of Charlemagne,
when kings would gird on the sword of a promising young warrior, who
took rank above the mass by riding on horseback. The warhorse was ever
the essential instrument of the son of chivalry.

In the eleventh century Knighthood had become an established and well
defined institution in western Europe, particularly in France. It was feudal
France that produced the ethos of chivalry, its ritual in fealty (fidelity of a
vassal to his lord) and Knighthood, its symbols in heraldry, its diversions in
the hunt and the tournament. The word 'chivalry' comes from the old
French *chevalerie*, for horsemanship, and from this we get 'cavalry' and
'cavalier'. After victory at Hastings in 1066 the Normans established
Feudalism and its attendant chivalry in England. The name 'knight' derives
from the Anglo-Saxon *cnicht*, a servant of the king.

The Crusades gave a powerful impulse and a more religious turn to the spirit of chivalry and made the knights of all the Christian nations known to each other so that a great uniformity developed among them throughout Europe. The Crusades gave rise to the religious military orders – the Knights Templar, the Knights of St John, and the Teutonic Knights (see Chapter Five, THE CRUSADES). The laws of chivalry became widely recognized and enforced and were submitted to by every man who desired to win both the love of women and honourable fame among men.

The training of an aspirant knight began at the age of about ten, when the boy was sent to the court of a lord or baron to spend several years as a page, carrying out practical household duties and physical exercises. He waited on the lord and his lady at table and accompanied them on the hunt. He received religious instruction from the chaplain, basic weapon training from the squires, and was taught by his mistress to honour and protect all women. He also learned to sing, to play the lute, and to dance, for it was a duty to provide entertainment. He learned to manage hound and hawk, but above all else he learned to master horsemanship.

At the age of fourteen the page became a knight's squire or 'esquire', from *escuyer*, a word generally supposed to be derived from *scutum*, a shield, for one of the squire's duties was to carry the shield of the knight whom he served. The youth now began a regular training for arms and battle. On

HUYOT

Tilting at the quintain, target practice for esquire and knight.

A new knight receiving the
accolade.

Buckling on the spurs of a new knight. Spurs were a potent symbol of chivalry.

horseback he tilted at the 'quintain', an upright post with a pivoted crossbar at the top; on one end of the bar was suspended a bag of sand, the other end was broad and flat, sometimes with a shield serving as a target. He rode tilt at the target with his lance and endeavoured to strike it and pass on before the bag of sand could swing round and hit him on the back.

The squire attended his knight in hall and field and accompanied him to war, assisted him in putting on his armour, caring for his weapons and horses. He stood by to give aid in battle should his knight be overmatched, and to give his mount should his master lose his own. It was the squire who raised his knight when he fell and who bore his body away if wounded or killed in battle or tournament.

At the age of twenty-one, having acquitted himself well, the squire was admitted to Knighthood. There were, however, exceptions to the rule for those of distinguished birth: Edward the Black Prince, son of Edward III, was made a knight at sixteen. The ceremony of Knighthood was elaborate and solemn. The candidate prepared himself for his new dignity by long vigils, fasts, and prayer; on the eve of the ceremony he remained alone in the church before the altar on which lay the precious armour he would don the next day.

In the morning high mass was performed in the presence of the nobles, bishops, and an assembly of people. After the sword of the novice had been consecrated to the service of heaven he took a solemn vow according to the laws of chivalry – to speak the truth, to defend the church, to succour the helpless and oppressed, to protect women and orphans, to live in harmony

A knight in complete armour, period 1461–1480. He is wearing a tabard, a short surcoat emblazoned with his heraldic emblems. His helmet is the great bascinet adorned with plume.

with his equals, never to retreat before the enemy, et cetera (the French had twenty vows of Knighthood). He then received the 'accolade', a symbolic blow on the neck from either the hand or the flat of the sword of the person who dubbed him knight. In the early period any knight could bestow Knighthood, in later years it was only given by a great lord or the monarch. Other knights, and often the ladies present, buckled on the new knight's armour. The spurs were usually put on first and thus came to be regarded as the symbol of Knighthood. If convicted of cowardice or any dishonourable deed a knight had his spurs hacked off as a mark of degradation. At his burial, the spurs of a true knight were laid in the tomb beside him.

The new knight might ride off in search of adventure, a knight-errant seeking a just cause to serve. A knight-errant proclaimed himself as such by riding through the peaceful country in full armour, attended by a single squire. Some paladins genuinely tried to emulate the heroic deeds of the mythical knights of King Arthur's Round Table, or the knights of Charlemagne. Others served foreign kings in a mercenary capacity and were often rewarded with large estates.

Some became knights of renown by riding from tournament to tournament, winning rich prizes and acquiring the armour and horses of the fellow-knights they defeated in the martial contests. William Marshal (c.1146–1219) – who later became regent of England for the infant Henry III – spent several years as a young knight travelling through northern

A knight of the 15th century rides off to war.

A tournament, or mock battle between knights.

France, fighting in tournaments. He won great fame and fortune; in one tournament alone he bested twelve knights.

The tournament was immensely popular with the knights and the public, spectacular gladiatorial competition and fun-fair combined. The contests took place in the 'lists', an open space around which stands would be erected for the spectators. 'Tournament' (from the French *tourner*, 'to turn round') is the name generally given to embrace all the combative sports in which knights encountered each other with either blunted weapons or sharp, in order to display their skill at arms.

However, the tournament proper, or *mêlèe*, was a spirited battle in which two parties of knights clashed in massed combat, and in the early years deaths and injuries often resulted. The 'joust' (from the French *joute*, for contest) was a fight between two knights, the defeated man being obliged to yield his horse and armour to the victor. The combatants used lance, sword, mace or axe. Because of the many fatalities incurred, the church and a number of monarchs discouraged the sport but it continued, albeit in a

less dangerous form. The 'barrier' or 'tilt' was introduced in which two knights rode at each other on either side of a wooden barrier with the object of unseating the other with levelled lance. Special armour strengthened on the left side was developed for this contest. In France the death of Henry II, accidentally killed in a tournament by Count Montgomery in 1559, hastened the abolition of the knightly sport.

The duel of chivalry was a fight to the death to settle a point of honour, and only rarely was mercy shown by the victor to the vanquished in such a bitter combat. An example of chivalric magnanimity occured in 1390 at the conclusion of a duel between the Scottish knight Sir David de Lindsay and the English noble, John, Lord Welles. The fight arose over an argument as to who were the more courageous, the Scots or the English. The conflict took place on Old London Bridge before King Richard II and a large crowd.

The two knights rode at each other full tilt; both broke their lances on the first impact, but neither was hurt. In the second course they again shattered their lances without inflicting any great injury. They charged a third time and Lord Welles was knocked from the saddle and lay stunned on the ground. Sir David swiftly dismounted and knelt beside the fallen man. The crowd expected him to deliver the traditional *coup de grâce* with his dagger through his adversary's open visor. But he did not do so. He removed his opponent's helmet and tended him gently until Lord Welles's squires carried him away for treatment. Sir David's chivalrous act was much admired by the king and

Knights jousting with lances tipped with a special prong device to prevent fatalities.

the public. The last duel of chivalry in England took place in 1492 between Sir James Parker and Sir Hugh Vaughan; Parker was killed in the first charge, his helmet broke before Vaughan's lance and 'he was so stricken into the mouth that his tongue was borne into the hinder part of his head'.

A knight-bachelor (one who served under the banner of another) rode into battle carrying a swallow-tailed pennon on his lance which bore his heraldic device. A squire carried a lance with a triangular 'penoncel' or 'pencel' adorned with his emblem or that of his chief. If a knight-bachelor distinguished himself in action he might be elevated to a knight-banneret on the battlefield; he presented his pennon to the king or commander, who cut off the swallow-tail making it square. Bannerets were sometimes called knights of the square banner, marking authority over a force of men capable of forming a solid square of from ten to fifteen men per face, hence the term 'squadron'.

It is interesting to note that at the time of Crécy, 1346, a knight-banneret was paid four shillings a day; a knight-bachelor two shillings a day; a squire a shilling a day, and a man-at-arms (a fully armoured horseman but not a knight) sixpence a day. In the fourteenth century the military term 'men-at-arms' also included knights.

A knight of the late Middle Ages, the apogee of chivalry, wore plate armour from head to foot, 'cap-à-pie', as it was called. He charged into battle on a tall, heavy horse, seated securely in a saddle with high pommel and cantle; he rode with a straight leg and long stirrup, a stand-up style which gave him greater striking power with his couched lance, and enabled him to wield his sword or axe with more agility.

A knight would not cross swords with a foot-soldier out of choice, only if under immediate attack. Knight fought knight. The French sons of chivalry held foot-soldiers in utter contempt and were wont to ride down their own infantry if they got in the way. It is said that Edward III was quite upset on learning that his low-born Welsh and Irish spearmen had killed many dismounted French knights with daggers as they lay stunned or wounded on the field of Crécy. When one knight yielded to another he was usually held for ransom, and while held captive was well treated according to the code of chivalry.

However, a fight between knights in the heat of battle was a savage, desperate affair. Sir John Chandos, serving under Edward the Black Prince in Spain, pressed too far among the enemy in the battle of Najera, 1367, and was 'grappled by a huge Castillian knight of noted prowess, named Martin Fenant, and would have been slain had he not bethought himself a knife that was in the bosom of his surcoat. This he plunged repeatedly into the back and ribs of Martin as he lay above him [apparently the Spaniard had no back armour]; then he turned him over on his back, and started up just as his followers came to his rescue.' The dagger which knights employed in these close encounters was named, somewhat inaptly, the 'poinard of mercy'.

The duel of chivalry, single combat to the death in order to settle a point of honour. From a 15th-century MS.

‡ 63 ‡

Champion of the tournament,
his horse wearing the victor's
laurels on his head. After an
engraving by Albrecht Dürer.

In 1344 Edward III created the most distinguished order of English
Knighthood, the Order of the Garter, which originally consisted of the king
and twenty-six eminent knights, joined together by the vows of eternal
fidelity for the 'advancement of piety, nobility, and chivalry'. The king
chose for the Order's badge and name a lady's garter, dropped by mischance
at a banquet by the beautiful princess Joan of Kent. Edward picked up the
garter and tied it round his knee, with the comment, '*Honi soit qui mal y
pense*' ('Evil be to him who thinks evil of it'), and this became the official
motto of the Order, the badge of which is a royal blue garter embroidered
with the motto and the cross of St George. The Order of the Bath was

A later development of the joust was the introduction of the barrier, a wooden fence that separated the contestants to prevent a serious collision.

instituted in 1399 by Henry IV of England and got its name from the ritual bathing of the candidate on initiation in token of the purity required by members of the Order.

The office of 'herald' as established in the Middle Ages was essentially a chivalric institution and derived its importance from the customs of Knighthood. Heralds began to appear in the twelfth century. At first they were mere couriers of low rank, later they were chosen from the Knighthood. The functions of a herald were to carry messages of courtesy or defiance between monarchs or persons of high rank, to superintend and register the results of tournaments, to record the valiant deeds of combatants, to proclaim war or peace, to identify (from their heraldic emblems) and compute the dead knights after battle, marshal processions and public ceremonials, and especially to regulate and determine all matters connected with the use of armorial bearings. The College of Arms, which controls heraldry in England today, was founded by Richard III in 1483.

Four leaders of the First Crusade. Godfrey of Bouillon, his brother Baldwin, Raymond of Toulouse, and Bohemond of Tarentum.

Chapter Five T THE CRUSADES

HE CRUSADES were the military expedi-
tions undertaken by the Christian nations of western Europe against the
Moslems, from the end of the eleventh to the close of the thirteenth century,
for the recovery of Jerusalem and the Holy Land (Palestine) from the power
of the Saracens. They were called Crusades because the soldiers serving the
Christian cause wore the sign of the cross (*crux*, in Latin). The name 'Saracen'
(from the Byzantine Greek *sarakēnos*) was the generic term applied by
Europeans to all Eastern people of the Moslem faith.

The noble ideals of the crusaders were soon debased by their merciless
cruelty, greed, and self-aggrandizement. On many occasions they behaved
more brutally than their so-called barbarous enemies. To slaughter Saracens
was regarded as a laudable and necessary act and there were thousands of
Christian warriors eager to wade in Moslem blood with the battle cry
Deus lo volt! (God wills it!)

To the Christians of Europe, Jerusalem was a holy place of pilgrimage;
the tomb of Christ, the Mount of Olives, Golgotha, and all places and things
associated with the life and death of Christ were so sacred that they were
believed to possess divine powers of healing and forgiveness. In 1071 the

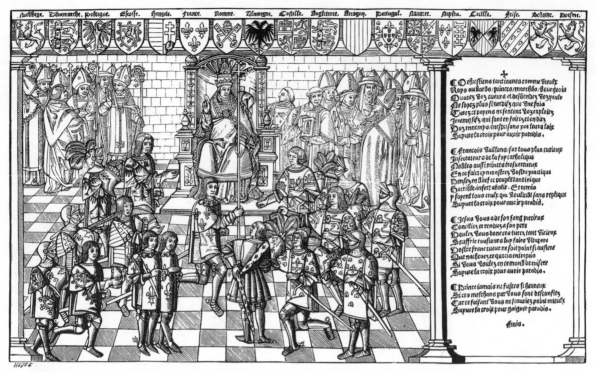

Pope Urban II convened a council at Clermont, France, in 1095 and proclaimed the First Crusade. A representation of the scene printed in 1522 with the crusader knights wearing 16th-century armour.

fierce Seljuk Turks of Asia Minor captured Jerusalem from the tolerant Fatimid caliphs of Cairo, and returning Christian pilgrims brought back tales of persecution by the Turks.

It must be said that it is not certain that the Seljuks did in fact maltreat the pilgrims, but it was believed so in Europe and that was enough to arouse the Christian nations. In 1095 Pope Urban II convened a council at Clermont in central France and pleaded for an armed expedition to rescue the holy places of Jerusalem from the infidel Saracens. All those who should march on such an expedition were promised complete remission of sins and eternal reward in heaven. Where religious zeal was not sufficient motive, the attractions of warfare, plunder, and the acquisition of foreign estates served as powerful magnets. The badge of the cross was taken up by all sorts and conditions of men – kings, princes, bishops, knights, and poor peasants.

The proper military preparations of the crusader nobles and knights lasted too long for the impatience of the excited, common people, who set out in the spring of 1096, a disorderly rabble of some 500,000 French, Germans, and Italians led by Peter the Hermit (a leading preacher of the First Crusade) and a poor knight known as Walter the Penniless. The sanctified mob marched through Germany to Hungary *en route* to Constantinople, bastion of the Greek Christian Byzantine Empire. When refused provisions by the people whose lands they travelled through, the crusaders looted, raped, and murdered. They in turn were attacked and thousands were killed. On reaching Constantinople, the ragged army so dismayed Alexius Comnenus, the Greek emperor, that he hastily shipped them across the Bosporus to Asia Minor, where they were slaughtered by the Seljuks without ever reaching Jerusalem.

The organized forces of warrior crusaders, numbering some 400,000 knights and foot-soldiers, arrived in Constantinople in May 1097. They were mostly French, Norman, and Flemish commanded by Godfrey of Bouillon, Duke of Lorraine, and his brother Baldwin; Robert II of Normandy, eldest son of William the Conqueror; Hugh of Vermandois, brother of the King of France; Raymond of Toulouse, Bohemond of Tarentum and his cousin Tancred of Apulia, and other experienced commanders of elevated

Knights and a foot-soldier of the First Crusade. The foot-soldier boasts a mail coif, or hood, his only armour.

‡69‡

The light-mounted Saracen was no match for the heavy crusader knight in close combat. On the other hand, the Frank horseman could never catch a Turk or match his agility on a swift Arab steed.

rank. Because the First Crusade was largely French in character the Saracens came to refer to all crusaders as 'Franks'.

Knights of the First Crusade wore mail armour much the same as that worn by the Norman knight in 1066: a knee-length hauberk (chain mail shirt) with elbow-length sleeves, worn over a gambeson (tunic) of linen or wool. Helmets were mostly conical with a nasal or nose-piece; later crusaders wore a flat-topped helm which completely covered the face. Shields were long and kite-shaped to give maximum protection on a horse. Weapons included the sword, lance, mace or axe. Ordinary foot-soldiers were forbidden the knightly sword. The crusading chivalry soon adopted the Saracen custom of wearing a loose linen coat (surcoat) over their armour to lessen the effect of the desert sun on metal.

Saracen horsemen also wore chain mail suits, but of a lighter more flexible kind. Their mounts were lighter, smaller, swifter than those of the Christian knights. The Turkish horse-archers used a shortbow of composite make, whereas the crusaders favoured the crossbow. The Saracens employed nimble, hit-and-run tactics and were masters of the ambush. When faced with a spirited headlong crusader charge, the resilient Moslems would melt before it, wheel away swiftly and punish the Christian flanks with arrows. The heavy mounted European knight could usually best a Saracen horseman in close combat, but could never catch a Turk or match his agility on an Arab steed at the gallop.

Having reluctantly taken the oath of fealty to the Byzantine Emperor and promised to restore to him the territory now occupied by the Seljuks, the crusaders were transported across the Bosporus by Alexius into Asia

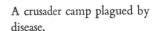

Minor. In June 1097 they captured the city of Nicea after a seven-week siege and early in July met the Turks in open battle for the first time. A separate column under Bohemond was surrounded by a vast army of 300,000 Saracens on the plain of Dorylaeum. The Christian knights charged directly at the massed Turkish horsemen, expecting them to stand and fight in the European manner.

But the heathen warriors scattered before the onslaught of the heavy cavalry, denying the Franks the satisfaction of a shock impact. The fast-moving Turks now battered the knights with showers of arrows. Again and again the Christian cavalry attempted to bring the elusive enemy to close combat, but the Turks refused to come to sword strokes, preferring to fight at arrow distance. With many of their horses killed, the crusaders found themselves in a desperate situation, facing defeat. Bohemond sent riders through the Saracen ring to get help from the forces commanded by Godfrey of Bouillon and Raymond of Toulouse, who arrived just in time to save their surrounded comrades. The Turks, badly hammered, faded away in defeat.

The crusaders marched on through Asia Minor. Baldwin now parted company with the Christian army to pursue a personal career of conquest; he crossed the Euphrates, seized the city of Edessa and established an independent state. In late October 1097 the crusaders besieged the great fortified city of Antioch, which was well provisioned and ably defended by the Seljuk emir Yagi Siyan. As the siege dragged on (it lasted nine months) and

When the crusaders first looked upon the holy city of Jerusalem in 1099 they fell to their knees and gave thanks to God.

winter came, the Christian army suffered in such extreme that desertions were frequent; many died of famine, many others of disease and exhaustion. The crusaders were thinned to an alarming degree.

Unable to obtain any other kind of food, the humbler crusaders turned to cannibalism, making the most of any Saracens they killed. The horses suffered equally with their knight-masters and in a few months the total number of mounts was reduced from more than 70,000 to a mere 2,000. Unusually heavy rains turned the whole camp into a morass; tents rotted and decayed in the wet, and the position soon presented the appearance of a vast graveyard.

Then Antioch, with the exception of the inner citadel, was delivered to the crusaders by a Saracen traitor, an emir who commanded the outer wall; the gates were opened on 3 June 1098, the Franks swarmed in and massacred all they could find in the streets and houses. However, before they could

The crusaders chose Godfrey
to be King of Jerusalem, but
he refused the crown and
assumed the title of Protector
of the Holy Sepulchre.

take the citadel, the crusaders were themselves besieged by a newly arrived army commanded by Kerboga, Emir of Mosul. The Christians were soon reduced to the utmost extremity by hunger and pestilence. They were saved by what seemed a miracle.

Inside Antioch a priest named Peter Bartholomew claimed to have had a vision in which a holy figure told him that the Roman lance which had pierced Christ's side as he hung from the cross was buried in Antioch's church of St Peter, and that victory would come to the soldiers who carried the holy relic into battle. The desperate crusaders dug in the church and did indeed unearth a rusty spear head, which they accepted without question as the Holy Lance. Convinced now of victory, the Christians marched out and attacked the besieging Turks with such fanatical frenzy that the Saracens fled the field in a demoralized state.

On learning of Kerboga's defeat, the inner citadel surrendered. Throughout the long siege the Frank commanders, rivals in grabbing power and prestige, had bickered and quarrelled (as other leaders were to do in future Crusades). Now that the city was taken a bitter argument arose between Bohemond and Raymond of Toulouse as to who would be Prince of Antioch. After resting there for six months, the main crusader army marched on to their chief objective, Jerusalem. Bohemond, however, remained at Antioch with his men and established another independent principality.

The Christian army, now reduced to some 25,000 under the command of Godfrey of Bouillon, began the siege of Jerusalem on 7 June 1099. After stiff resistance on the part of the defenders and the most violent exertions by the attackers, the city was taken by storm on 15 July with the aid of two tall siege towers (see Chapter Seven, SIEGES AND SIEGE MACHINES). The blood-crazed crusaders sealed their victory with a dreadful massacre of the inhabitants, men, women and children, an atrocity such as the Turk had not been guilty of in his most savage moments. After the butchery the Christian warriors walked barefooted and bareheaded and knelt at the Holy Sepulchre.

The crusaders chose Godfrey to be King of Jerusalem but, legend tells us, he wisely refused, saying: 'I cannot wear a crown of gold in the city where Jesus had worn a crown of thorns.' Instead, he styled himself Protector of the Holy Sepulchre. When Godfrey died in July 1100 he was succeeded by his brother Baldwin, who eagerly accepted the crown which Godfrey had refused. The territory over which he ruled consisted merely of the cities of Jerusalem and Jaffa (Joppa), together with some minor towns and about twenty villages. During the reign of Baldwin I (1100–1118) the boundaries

of the Kingdom of Jerusalem were extended considerably. He died during
an expedition into Egypt and was succeeded by Baldwin II who occupied
the throne for thirteen years and further extended the Christian realm by the
sword.

The Kingdom of Jerusalem and the question of its permanent defence gave
rise to two great orders of Knighthood, the Knights Hospitaller and the
Knights Templar, described by Henry Treece in *The Crusades* (1962) as
'spiritual warriors or fighting-monks; a race set apart from all others, to
form the military striking-force of the whole area about Jerusalem'. Originally a monastic order founded to succour Christian pilgrims in the Holy
Land, the Hospitallers became a military order in 1118; it still retained
brothers solely devoted to charitable services, but it now had a martial
brotherhood known as the Knights of St John of Jerusalem, who became
celebrated warriors of fearsome renown. They wore a white cross on a red
tunic.

The Knights Templar, a similar order to the above, was founded in 1123

The Knights Templar were fierce warrior-monks who also served as a standing army for Jerusalem. They wore a red cross on a white tunic.

for the protection of pilgrims on the roads of the Holy Land. Baldwin II gave them quarters near the old Temple of Solomon, hence their name 'soldiers of the temple' or Templars. They wore a red cross on a white tunic. And like the Knights of St John they also became soldiers of great fame. Their martial exploits attracted recruits from all over Europe, also rich donations and legacies. The Templars and the Knights of St John took vows of obedience to a Grand Master, whom they appointed, and bound themselves to chastity.

These fierce fighting-monks served as the standing army of the Kingdom of Jerusalem, an experienced force to supplement the transient crusading armies from Europe. They manned castles along the border, one of the most notable being the formidable Krak des Chevaliers of the Hospitallers. In battle they neither gave nor asked for quarter and seldom received mercy from the Saracens when captured. Another religious order on the same pattern was that of the Teutonic Knights, founded in 1190 for Germans of noble rank. The original object of the order being the defence of Christianity

‡77‡

and the care of the sick in the Holy Land. In the thirteenth century the Teutonic Knights, who wore a black cross on a white tunic, undertook the conquest and conversion by the sword of the heathen Prussians, and acquired much territory in the southern Baltic regions.

The Second Crusade, provoked by the loss of Edessa to the Seljuk Turks in 1144, was a failure. The German emperor Conrad III and Louis VII of France set out to defend the cross in 1147, but the stately expedition proved fruitless and returned to Europe in 1149, leaving the Kingdom of Jerusalem in a much weaker condition than they had found it. Twenty years later Saladin, greatest of all Saracen leaders, became the Sultan of Egypt and he inspired a Moslem Holy War, or *Jehad* against the Christians with the object of recapturing the city of Jerusalem.

The Third Crusade, 1189–1192, was put into motion when Saladin succeeded in taking Jerusalem in 1187. The three most powerful kings of Europe, Frederick I of Germany, Philip Augustus of France, and Richard I ('Coeur de Lion') of England 'took the cross' and personally led their crusading armies against the infidels. Frederick, known as 'Barbarossa' from his red beard, was an aged but able general and all went well with the Germans, who defeated a large Turkish army near Iconium in May 1190,

The Hospitallers and the Templars manned castles along the border of the Christian kingdom. The celebrated Krak des Chevaliers in Syria, shown here, was a stronghold of the Hospitallers.

till the old emperor was drowned in a stream in Asia Minor, then the German expedition fell apart.

When Richard and Philip arrived in the Holy Land they found the Christians besieging the city of Acre. After a weary siege of twenty-three months the city was taken. But Richard and Philip quarrelled and the French king soon returned home. Richard, a magnificent fighting man, acted with supreme arrogance and indifference to his allies (and in his dealing with Saladin), almost to the point of stupidity.

The traditional view of Richard the Lion-Hearted is that of the crusader *par excellence*, a shining hero of courtly chivalry and knightly behaviour. His prodigious physical strength, personal courage, and military skills are beyond question. However, he was also treacherous and barbarous; in the words of Gibbon 'he united the ferocity of a gladiator to the cruelty of a tyrant'. He was a bad king, spending only six months of his reign (1189–1199) in England, taxing his people heavily to finance his military adventures. He was fit only for war.

Wrangling and jealousy was rife among the leaders of the Third Crusade. When Philip of France lay ill, Richard made cruel sport with him by bearing the false news that his only son, Louis, was dying. On taking Acre, Richard's ally Leopold of Austria ran up his banner from a high tower; Richard rashly tore it down, thus earning Leopold's undying enmity. Richard made a deal with Saladin to set free 2,700 Saracens captured at Acre for a large ransom payable within forty days. In raising the huge ransom, Saladin failed to deliver it within the stipulated period, whereupon Richard the cruel-hearted immediately slaughtered the prisoners. The Saracen leader never trusted Richard again. Saladin was everything that Richard was not – cultured, truly chivalrous, a man of his word, and merciful; when he captured Jerusalem he did not massacre his captives as did the crusaders when they took the city.

In the 13th century the Teutonic Knights embarked upon a Crusade against the heathen Prussians, the Poles and the Lithuanians.

Although the Third Crusade was a failure in that Jerusalem was not recaptured, the Christian expedition did enjoy several victories over the Turks, in particular Richard's triumph in the battle of Arsouf on 7 September 1191, in which his skill as a field commander and his ability to control

Richard the Lion-Heart was a magnificent warrior, a knight without peer in combat. He is shown here at the battle of Jaffa.

his men in adverse conditions were brilliantly displayed. Richard's advance on Jerusalem entailed an eighty-mile march along the coast from Acre to Jaffa, before turning inland for the Holy City.

Saladin harassed the crusaders all the way. But Richard had organized his army with considerable care. His order of march being also his order of battle. By keeping close to the shore he secured his right flank from attack, and his soldiers were maintained by supplies from the ships which accompanied the army. Two columns of infantry marched either side of the central column of knights, the Hospitallers and the Templars formed the van and rear guards, the baggage train marched closest to the shore. In this formation the foot-soldiers were able to protect the horses of the knights, who made sporadic but disciplined charges against the mounted Turkish archers.

Saladin's tactics, which had proved successful in previous encounters with the Franks, were to provoke the enemy into breaking their solid formation, to separate the knights from their safe infantry base, then destroy each force in detail. To accomplish this the Saracen horse-archers would sweep in close, bombard the crusaders with arrows, then ride off, hoping to draw a rash pursuit from the knights, who would then be overwhelmed by the main Turkish army. But Richard kept his men under firm control. Boha-ed-din, the Saracen chronicler, describes the situation:

‡81‡

Saladin, Sultan of Egypt, shown here receiving the Bishop of Salisbury and other Christian pilgrims.

'The enemy marched in order of battle, their infantry placed between us and their cavalry, keeping as level and firm as a wall. Each foot-soldier wore a thick cassock of felt, and under it a mail shirt so strong that our arrows made no impression on them. They, meanwhile, shot at us with crossbows, which struck down horse and man among the Moslems. I noted among them [the crusaders] men who had from one to ten shafts sticking in their backs, yet they trudged on at their ordinary pace and did not fall out of their ranks . . .

'The Franks continued to advance in this order, fighting vigorously all the way. The Moslems sent in volleys of arrows from all sides, endeavouring to irritate the knights into leaving their rampart of infantry. But it was all in vain. They kept their temper admirably and marched without hurrying themselves in the least, while their ships sailed along the coast parallel with them till they reached their camping place for the night. It was impossible not to admire the patience which these people showed.'

Having failed to divide Richard's army by provocation, Saladin decided on an all-out assault near the little town of Arsouf. This suited Richard and his knights; the light Saracen horse-soldier were no match for the heavy mounted crusaders. In answer to a trumpet signal, Richard's foot-soldiers

Richard executes 2,700 prisoners taken at Acre.

In the battle of Arsouf, 1191, Richard defeated the Saracens, whose swift-riding horse-archers are shown here harassing the column of marching crusaders.

opened their ranks to allow the knights, fresh for the fight, to charge out and meet the advancing enemy. They crashed into the tightly massed Saracens with tremendous impact, overturning horsemen in thousands. Brought to a shattered stop the Moslems, surprised by the unexpected counter-attack, turned and fled. Richard, aware of the danger of a long and scattered pursuit allowed his men only a short chase, then reformed his army. Discipline, an unusual element in medieval warfare, had won the day. Saladin never again attempted open battle with Richard.

Victory at Arsouf left the way open to Jerusalem. But Saladin, in adopting a 'scorched earth' policy and poisoning the wells, forced Richard to withdraw to the coast. Finally, despairing of ever taking Jerusalem, Richard concluded a three-year truce with Saladin, who agreed that Christian pilgrims should be freely permitted to visit the Holy Sepulchre and that the whole sea coast from Tyre to Jaffa (including the fortress of Acre) should remain in Christian hands. This treaty was made on 2 September 1192 and the following month Richard departed, saying: 'I will return in three years to conquer the Holy Land.' But he never did.

The chief result of the Third Crusade was the possession of Acre which, until the entire termination of the Crusades remained the bulwark of the Christians in the East. The Fourth Crusade, 1200–1204, never even reached the Holy Land. It was diverted from its original purpose and turned against Christian Constantinople to serve the political and economic interests of Henry Dandolo, the intriguing Doge of Venice, who hoped to gain considerable advantages for his independent mercantile city by the destruction of rival Constantinople, capital of the Byzantine Empire.

Baldwin, Count of Flanders, storming Constantinople during the mis-named and mis-directed Fourth Crusade.

The Seventh Crusade, 1248-1254, was led by Louis IX of France, represented in this curious print, published in 1522, landing at Damietta in Egypt. Here the 13th century crusaders are wearing 16th century dress.

The Fifth Crusade, 1218–1221, involved the invasion of Egypt. After the capture of Damietta, the crusaders were split by dissension and were obliged to come to a treaty with the Moslems and evacuate the Nile delta. Damietta was recaptured by the Sultan Malik-al-Kamil in 1221, by which the Crusade came to an end. The Sixth Crusade, 1228–1229, was a curious affair. It was undertaken by Frederick II of Germany, who, having caused displeasure to the Pope, had been excommunicated. Because of this other crusaders refused to join him. However, Frederick's own troops and the Teutonic Knights remained loyal. Without any fighting, Frederick made a treaty with Sultan al-Kamil, whereby he obtained the Holy City and crowned himself King of Jerusalem. Fifteen years later the Moslems were again masters of the disputed city.

The Seventh Crusade, 1248–1254, and the Eighth Crusade, 1270–1272, were both led by Louis IX of France. Having taken Damietta, he marched against Cairo but was defeated and captured in 1250. Louis recovered his freedom on the payment of a huge ransom and the surrender of Damietta; failing to re-establish the power of the Kingdom of Jerusalem, he returned

Les turs.

Louis IX also led the Eighth and last Crusade, 1270-1272. He is pictured in this print of 1518 landing at Carthage, near Tunis.

to France in 1254. During the Eighth and last Crusade, Louis died of a fever while besieging Tunis. Prince Edward of England (later Edward I) took part in this Crusade but achieved very little; he concluded a ten-year truce in 1272 and returned to England to assume the crown.

The capture of Acre in 1291 by the Sultan of Egypt, just 100 years after it had been taken by Richard I of England and Philip Augustus of France extinguished for ever the kingdom founded by the crusaders and terminated the age of the Crusades proper. Western Europe learned much from its contact with the Saracens, especially about fortifications and military architecture (see Chapter Six, CASTLES AND FORTIFICATIONS).

The keep of Richmond
Castle, a typical square
Norman keep.

Chapter Six

CASTLES AND FORTIFICATIONS

Castles were the bulwark of feudal society. A castle was the fortified residence of a monarch or lord. The western kingdoms of the Middle Ages were studded with numerous castles; they were the strongholds of military power, the chief points of defence, and often served as the keys to victory in war. Anchored on rocky crags high above rivers and valleys, they commanded roads, river fords or mountain passes, protecting and at the same time oppressing the poor peasants who lived in the villages within the castle's shadow.

The word 'castle' comes from the Latin *castellum*, a diminutive of *castrum*, a fortress or stronghold. *Castellum* was used by the Romans as a military term for a small frontier fort, of which they built many in the territories they conquered. Thus a privately-owned fort not part of the defences of a town came to be called a castle.

In the early Middle Ages, Charlemagne (768–814) developed a system of frontier posts in the Roman manner to protect his Frankish Empire from Viking and other barbarian raiders; in the ninth century Frankish dominion covered most of western Europe. When the empire of the Franks dissolved, the forts became the residences of local warlords. This type of early castle consisted of a wooden tower erected on a mound of earth, surrounded by a broad ditch and palisade.

When the Northmen raiders settled in France and became the Normans of Normandy, they absorbed the Frankish concept of the castle as the instrument of defence and subjection. In England, the private fortress was virtually unknown before the Norman invasion. To protect themselves from marauders the English built communal 'burhs', settlements surrounded by earthworks and stockades, in which all the people could shelter in times of danger. From 'burh' came the word 'borough' meaning a township.

When William of Normandy landed in England in 1066 he brought with him several wooden castles 'framed and prepared beforehand'. To consolidate his occupation of England, William erected hundreds of wood and earth castles all over the land, particularly near Anglo-Saxon towns. The castles housed the Norman lords and knights who had been rewarded by William with estates taken from the people. The lords or barons remained in the service of the king and furnished troops for the royal army in time of war. Feudalism had taken root in England.

These early Norman castles were constructed on the 'motte and bailey'

Castle of the motte-and-bailey type built on a headland for additional protection. The stone keep is surrounded by a wooden wall.

system. The wooden tower, encircled by a palisade, was placed on a high mound ('motte') of earth, surrounded by a deep ditch from which the mound was dug. Below the motte lay a large circular enclosure (the 'bailey'), also surrounded by a ditch and palisade. The motte was connected to the bailey by a removable bridge. The lord and his family lived in the motte tower while the soldiers, horses, cattle, kitchen and stores were lodged in the bailey area.

As time passed the wood and earth strongholds gave way to permanent stone structures, based on the motte and bailey principle, and the massive Norman 'keep' was established. In the twelfth century the keep or *donjon* developed into a several-storied square tower surrounded by thick stone walls which enclosed the bailey. The ground floor of the *donjon*, which had no doors and only a few tiny windows, contained the stores, well, armoury, and a prison (whence 'dungeon').

The ruins of Château Gaillard, built on a commanding loop of the Seine by Richard I of England to protect Rouen, capital of his Duchy of Normandy.

Saracen castle in Syria. Note the concentric design and curtain walls strengthened by projecting towers.

The floors above were occupied by the lord, his family and retainers. The first floor was reached by a broad flight of steps rising from the ground outside. The doorway led into a great hall which was used for entertaining. The main entrance of the bailey was made secure by a fortified gatehouse that contained a heavy, vertical-dropping grate called a 'portcullis', and a moveable drawbridge which spanned the moat. The keep was the centre of the castle complex to which the defenders retreated only in the last extremity, and was so strongly constructed that in many ruined castles it alone has survived. Splendid examples of twelfth-century Norman keeps are the White Tower of the Tower of London, Castle Hedingham in Essex, Norwich Castle, Rochester Castle, and Richmond Castle in Yorkshire.

As the corners of a square tower were vulnerable to undermining during a siege, the rectangular keep gave way to the round tower which was not so easily undermined. And an extra outer bailey was added for further protec-

A tower with machicolation, a projecting wall walk with openings looking straight down to the foot of the tower, enabling defenders to drop rocks or shoot arrows at the attackers immediately below.

tion. It is claimed that Henry II of England (1154–1189) was the first to build round tower keeps. The military experience gained by the Crusaders in the East revolutionized castle building in Europe. The Crusaders were impressed and influenced by the Byzantine fortified cities and the Saracen strongholds constructed on the concentric pattern.

Richard I of England (1189–1199) was a notable Crusader and skilled military engineer. He built one of the most celebrated and formidable of medieval castles, the Château Gaillard, to protect Rouen, the capital of his Duchy of Normandy against the attacks of King Philip Augustus of France. Richard sited his *magnum opus* on a commanding position in a loop of the Seine at Gaillon, on a spur of chalk hills which only a narrow neck of land connects with the general plateau. There, 300 feet above the river, he completed the great fortress in the remarkably short time of two years, between 1196 and 1198.

Richard incorporated eastern ideas in the château, securing the inner strongpoint with stout outer walls, each section flanked by projecting towers. So pleased was the king with his handiwork that he referred to it as his *Bellum Castrum de Rupe* – his 'Fair Castle of the Rock'.

The configuration of the Château Gaillard followed the contours of its clifftop site and, from a bird's eye view, took the rough shape of a ship. The pointed 'bows' contained the outer bailey, a separate unit completely enclosed by walls strengthened with round towers and surrounded by a moat. A bridge across the moat gave entry to the 'midships' of the middle bailey, also protected by high walls with towers.

Caernarvon Castle, a magnificent stronghold built by Edward I to command the entrance of the Menai Strait. Started in 1283 it was completed in 1323. This photograph was taken about 1920.

The middle bailey enclosed the inner bailey, the latter surrounded by walls and a moat contained the keep. The defences were interlocked, one after the other, in the only direction from which an assault could come. However, this seemingly impregnable fortress was taken by force in 1204 by Philip of France (see Chapter Seven, SIEGES AND SIEGE MACHINES). It might have been different if the lion-hearted Richard had been there to defend his beloved stronghold, but he had been killed while besieging the castle of Chalus in 1199. The Château Gaillard was destroyed in 1603 by Henry IV of France to curb the power of the Norman barons.

The reign of Edward I of England (1272–1307) was a busy time of castle building and during this period the castle, in architectural terms, reached its zenith. Mostly constructed on the concentric pattern, the Edwardian castles rose four-square with massive round towers at each corner connected by high curtain walls topped with crenellated battlements.

The typical Edwardian castle abandoned the keep as the main centre of defence and concentrated on two or three lines of defence disposed concentrically around the inner ward or bailey. The inner and outer walls were strengthened by a series of towers, usually circular or multiangular, projecting both outwards and inwards from the walls; these towers were all capable of being defended independently. From the jutting towers and the high wall battlements, bowmen shooting through arrow-loops could enfilade attackers from all directions.

The mighty four-towered gatehouse of Harlech Castle, another monument to Edward I, built between 1283 and 1290. This gatehouse boasted three great doors and three portcullises.

The towered gatehouses which guarded the main entrances were massive structures. Here lived the lord or the constable commanding the castle. The gatehouse incorporated a 'barbican', a walled passage leading from the inner gate to the outer gate and drawbridge. If the enemy broke through the outer gate they had the passage to contend with to reach the inner gate. The walls of the passage were pierced with loop holes and overhead were funnels for pouring down boiling liquids upon the assailants. Both outer and inner gates were fitted with portcullises.

Another architectural development which provided additional defence was that of machicolation. This took the form of wall-walks supported by 'corbels' or blocks of stone projecting from the wall with holes at regular intervals; this enabled the defenders to look down directly at the foot of the walls, and to shoot arrows, drop rocks, or pour boiling liquids upon the attackers.

Of the eight castles erected by Edward I to subdue the wild Welsh, those of Caernarvon, Conway, Harlech, Caerphilly, and Beaumaris are regarded as the finest and grandest in western Europe. Caernarvon Castle, started in 1283 and completed in 1323, was sited to command the entrance of the Menai Strait. It consisted of an upper and lower bailey enclosed by a curtain wall interspersed by nine major polygonal towers of six, eight and ten sides. In 1284 the future Edward II was born in the castle and was known as Edward of Caernarvon. The Welsh captured the partly-built fortress in 1294 but in its completed form it frustrated the attempts of Owen Glendower to take it in 1401 and 1404.

Harlech Castle stands on a headland 200 feet above sea level overlooking Tremadoc Bay. Made of local grey sandstone and built between 1283 and 1290, its four walls form a rectangle, each corner guarded by a mighty tower. Here can be seen a magnificent example of a four-towered gatehouse, a self-contained strongpoint, originally fitted with three great doors and three portcullises. Glendower captured the castle in 1401, and during the Wars of the Roses its Lancastrian defenders held the Yorkists at bay for eight years, thus inspiring the stirring march 'Men of Harlech'.

Beaumaris Castle was the last of Edward's strongholds to be built in Wales. Started in 1295 it was never fully completed. Sited on a marshy flat in Anglesey, close to the sea, this perfect example of the concentric castle was surrounded by a water-filled moat. It has inner and outer curtain walls, the inner being higher than the outer, the latter pierced with numerous loop-holes and braced with a dozen projecting towers. The great rectangular inner

‡96‡

The development of heavy guns ended the castle's role as a bastion. Later castles, like this French château built in the late 15th century, were more palatial residences than spartan strongholds.

curtain – sixteen feet thick – has six huge towers and two massive gatehouses, set in the centres of the north and south walls. Beaumaris and other Edwardian castles still stand today, impressive monuments to the Middle Ages.

Castles reached a peak of perfection and prominence in the late thirteenth and early fourteenth centuries and thereafter declined in military importance. With fortresses so powerful in defence and so costly to attack, campaigns were increasingly fought in the open. Finally, the advent of heavy guns ended the castle's key role as a bastion. Few new castles were built in the fourteenth and fifteenth centuries, and in those that were the trend was more for comfortable living than spartan defence. They developed into palatial residences, prestige seats of noblemen who still harboured outdated notions of chivalry. The castle had become a status symbol with no military value.

The new style fortifications of the fifteenth and sixteenth centuries were not intended as residences and therefore cannot be called castles. They were low-profiled gun forts designed to house artillery.

Chapter Seven SIEGES AND SIEGE
MACHINES

Dᴜʀɪɴɢ ᴛʜᴇ Middle Ages castles and
fortified cities were always under siege. The investing army would employ
various methods and machines in order to capture a walled city or stronghold, and the defenders would take the appropriate counter-measures to try
and foil the attackers. It would seem that the easiest way of bringing about
the surrender of a citadel would be to surround the place and starve its
defenders into submission. But this protracted approach was fraught with
difficulties.

A relief force might arrive to do battle with the besiegers. Disease could
break out and decimate the investing army. It was also possible that the
attackers might run out of supplies before the besieged; if the fortress was
well defended and well provisioned it could hold out for months, even years.
Another factor was the boredom induced by sitting and waiting for starv-
ation to win the day. There was also the difficulty of keeping a feudal army
together in the field for a long period. Therefore commanders usually
preferred to attempt to storm the place they were besieging.

Medieval sieges were conducted in similar manner to those of ancient
times. The so called 'engines' of war employed to batter and bombard the

‡99‡

walls were little different from those of classical antiquity used by the Greeks and Romans. The besieging commander would first surround the citadel and call upon its occupants to surrender. If met with refusal he would then decide on the tactics for capturing the place. He could either attempt an immediate attack using scaling ladders ('escalade'), or construct engines of bombardment, or set about undermining the walls, or wait and starve out the defenders. Often all these means were employed to bring a city to its knees.

An escalade would be mounted at several points at the same time in order to fragment the attention of the defenders, the attackers using wooden ladders fitted with hooks or clamps at the top for gripping the parapet. If a water-filled moat surrounded the stronghold, the attackers would have to construct rafts, bridges or a causeway if the necessary timber was available. The conduct of a siege was determined by the prevailing conditions and the natural resources at hand.

As the scaling parties approached the walls they would be given covering fire by archers and crossbowmen, who protected themselves in the open with large wooden shields called 'pavises' which they propped up while they fired their weapons. With the enemy climbing the ladders, the defenders would shower them with arrows, stones, boiling liquids, and quicklime, the latter intended to burn and blind. Forked poles would be used to push over the ladders, plunging the invaders to death or injury. If several escalades failed, the attacking commander would settle down to a siege proper.

In order to secure his encampment from a relieving force and from surprise sorties out of the stronghold he would dig outer and inner ditches strengthened by stockades. Castles and fortified cities had concealed posterns or small sally ports through which raiding parties could creep out at night to strike at the enemy camp, destroying supplies and siege machines. Thus protected on both sides the attacking commander would instruct his engineers and carpenters to build the various engines with which he could bombard the walls, and the stout moveable shelters under which his sappers could safely approach the walls to undermine or batter them. Again, such construction depended on the material available.

There were three main types of projectile-throwing machines. The 'mangonel' was a gigantic catapult, a legacy from the ancient Romans. It consisted of a central beam shaped like a spoon mounted on a strong, horizontal wooden frame. The base of the beam was rooted in a thick skein

The mangonel, a missile-throwing machine of ancient origin.

of ropes or sinews (the Romans preferred human hair for its greater elasticity). The skein was twisted towards the target by means of a windlass, thus forcing the beam hard upright against a crossbar. The beam was pulled back against the torsion and a large rock or other missile was placed in the cup or spoon end; when released the beam shot forward against the crossbar, catapulting its projectile with great velocity to distances up to 500 yards. Mangonels were made in various sizes and some were mounted on wheels or rollers.

The 'trebuchet' was a more powerful missile-throwing engine, first introduced in the latter part of the twelfth century, that worked by counterweight. A huge beam was fixed unevenly on the crossbar of an upright frame. The short end was heavily weighted with either one or two containers loaded with rocks. The longer, narrower end of the beam had a sling attached which carried the missile. The sling end was pulled down, then released; the heavier end dropped quickly, pivoting the sling upwards, which discharged its projectile with considerable force.

The mangonel and trebuchet could be employed to fling their missiles against walls to make a breach, or to hurl them right into the city streets or castle grounds. They were also used to throw the putrefying corpses of

Dramatic scene of trebuchet in action, used both by the besiegers and the defenders. Note barrel of Greek fire flying over the castle wall.

Two ways of breaching a wall, by battering-ram, and by giant screw or bore, the latter to pick away and loosen mortar and masonry.

horses or cattle into strongholds to spread disease, or containers of combustible mixtures, or the dreaded Greek fire, a flaming concoction of naptha and other stuff. Incendiary devices were also fixed to cats, dogs, and even birds to set fire to a besieged place.

The 'ballista', another weapon of ancient origin, was a monster crossbow fixed to a solid foundation; its propelling bowstring, pulled back by a windlass, could shoot large iron bolts, javelins, or stones with remarkable accuracy over several hundred yards. It was mainly used to pick off the enemy manning the walls and its arrow-like missile could transfix three men at the same time. Missile-throwing engines of the type mentioned were also used by the defenders.

The 'battering-ram' was a crude but effective device for smashing a breach in a wall or breaking down a gate or portcullis. It was simply a heavy tree trunk capped with iron (in many old prints it is shown decorated with a ram's head) and slung horizontally by ropes or chains from the roof of a long wooden canopy called a 'sow', which was rolled against the offending barrier. The team inside the sow swung the suspended ram repeatedly against the wall or gate until it gave way. The outer roof of the protective

shelter was covered in fresh animal hides to combat fire arrows or combustible mixtures from above. A giant screw or bore, a tree trunk fitted with a sharp iron point, was also used to pick away at mortar and masonry to effect a breach.

To counter the pounding action of the battering-ram, the defenders would lower wickerwork sections or padded buffers between the ram and its target area, or lower a heavy balk of timber on its protruding head. The surest way of stopping the ram was to drop great stones on the protective sow, crushing the canopy and its occupants. But stones of the required size were not always available. Sometimes a hook was lowered to catch the head of the ram and render it useless.

The undermining of walls and towers played a major role in siegecraft. The miners worked under the cover of a sow. As they dug under the foundations of a wall they shored up the excavated area with timber props. When they had burrowed sufficiently for their purpose, the sappers filled the tunnel with brushwood larded with animal fat, set fire to it and retired. The props would burn away and cause the wall above to collapse into the cavity.

King John used mining to good effect in capturing Rochester Castle in 1215. After besieging the rebel-held fortress for two months, John's soldiers

Lowering a balk of heavy timber on to the head of the battering-ram in order to negate its action. The balk could also be placed under the ram and, lifted, could render it ineffective.

managed to breach the bailey wall, whereupon the defenders withdrew to the great stone keep, 125 feet high. John ordered his sappers to drive a shaft under a corner of the square tower and sent a message, dated at Rochester on 25 November 1215, to Hubert de Burgh for animal fuel to feed the fire in the mine:

'We command you that with all haste, by day and by night, you send us 40 bacon pigs of the fattest and least good for eating, to bring fire under the tower.'

When the shaft was ready, the props and brushwood were covered in pig fat and fired. As planned, the corner of the keep came down and the king's men gained entry and finally captured the stronghold. Mining also brought about the downfall of Château Gaillard, the massive citadel in Normandy built by John's brother Richard I with a three-bailey defence.

King Philip of France laid siege to Château Gaillard in the late summer of 1203. He had once boasted that he would take the formidable castle 'even if its walls were made of iron'. To which the warrior King Richard had replied that he would hold it 'were its walls made of butter'. Alas, Richard was not there to defend it against Philip, having died in 1199. John attempted to relieve Château Gaillard but failed.

The siege continued throughout the winter and into the spring, when the French made a determined assault with mangonels and trebuchets; at the same time they made a causeway across the outer wet moat, undermined the outer bailey wall and breached it. Next came the middle bailey wall and this was also overcome. Then a section of the inner bailey wall was battered and mined until it collapsed, allowing the keep to be captured, the occupants of which were much weakened by hunger. The fall of the great stronghold led to the loss of Rouen and all of John's possessions in Normandy.

A castle built high on solid rock or surrounded by a broad water-filled moat had little to fear from undermining, but was not impregnable to a determined assault of that kind. Defenders of castles easily vulnerable to undermining could only thwart the enemy sappers by building a second rampart behind the wall under attack, or by digging a counter-mine down into the enemy tunnel to capture and fill it; both operations being difficult in time of siege.

If all the foregoing measures failed to gain entry into the citadel, another method of escalade could be attempted. Tall wooden towers, as high as the fortress walls, would be constructed. These 'belfries', as they were called, contained several apartments, one above the other, packed with storm troops

A siege tower, or 'belfry' was often used to get the besiegers over a castle wall. Note the cannon and the large shield, called a 'pavis', which protects the archers.

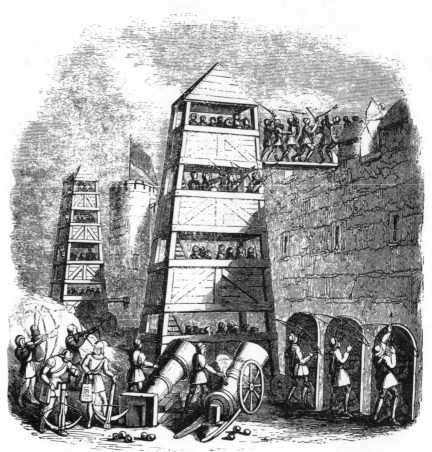

at each level, a ladder running from the ground floor to the top. The towers were wheeled or rolled against the wall, a drawbridge was lowered to span the gap and the attackers would charge over the parapet. William of Malmesbury, an English chronicler of the twelfth century, describes the use of a belfry by the Crusaders during the siege of Jerusalem in July 1099:

'The making of this machine delayed the siege, on account of the unskilfulness of the workmen and the scarcity of wood. And now the 14th day of July arrived when some men began to undermine the walls with the sows, others to move forward the tower. To do this more conveniently they took it towards the works in separate pieces and, putting it together at such distance as to be out of bow-shot, advanced it on wheels nearly close to the wall.

'In the meantime the slinger with stones, the archers and the crossbowmen began to press forward and dislodge their opponents from the ramparts.

‡ 108 ‡

A siege tower with a pivoted roof protection. Note the man in front of the castle wall using a hand-cannon.

Soldiers unmatched in courage ascend the tower, waging nearly equal war against the enemy with missile weapons and with stones. Nor indeed were our foes at all remiss; but trusting their whole security to their valour, they poured down grease and burning oil upon the tower . . . During the whole of that day the battle was such that neither army seemed to think they had been worsted.'

However, the next day some determined soldiers from the belfry managed to obtain a foothold upon the walls and those following swarmed into the city and opened one of the gates to let in the main army. Jerusalem was taken and the Crusaders exacted a terrible vengeance on the Turks for putting up such a fierce resistance, slaughtering some 40,000 of the city's inhabitants.

If frustrated in all his attempts to capture a stronghold by force of arms, the besieging commander had no alternative but to sit it out and starve the occupants into submission. The year-long siege of Calais by Edward III of England is a classic example of a properly organized investing army bringing a proud and powerful fortified city to abject surrender by hunger. The siege began on 31 August 1346.

Calais was immensely strong, surrounded by ditches and marsh lands; it supported a large garrison, was well provisioned and put up a spirited defence. King Edward realized that the city would not be taken in a hurry. He drew entrenchments round the place, had his soldiers build wooden huts thatched with straw or broom, and prepared by various means to render the winter campaign tolerable. His encampment of huts gave the appearance of a second town, called by the French chroniclers the *Ville du Bois*, the Town of Wood. Edward also blockaded the harbour to prevent the entrance of relief of any kind.

On viewing the king's intention of starving them out, John of Vienne, the governor of Calais, gathered all the inhabitants who were not necessary to the defence and sent 1,700 of them out of the city. Edward, to his credit, let them pass. But as the siege continued and John of Vienne again put out another 500 of what he considered useless mouths, Edward lost his patience and tolerance and refused them passage. The governor would not let them back into the city and the wretched refugees perished of hunger between the city walls and the English lines.

As the siege grew desperate, King Philip of France endeavoured to relieve the place. He sent ships to force a passage, but in vain. The English fleet of 700 ships dominated the Channel. Philip raised a large army and marched on the beleaguered city. The governor sent him urgent letters announcing that the inhabitants had eaten their horses, dogs and rats and unless relieved must soon eat each other. King Edward intercepted these letters but sent them on, taunting Philip by asking him why he did not come and relieve his sorely tried people.

But Philip found Edward so entrenched amongst the marshes and fortifications that he could not force a passage anywhere. Two roads only were left to the town – one along the seashore, and the other by a causeway through the marshes; but the coastway was completely raked by the English ships and boats, crowded with archers, and the causeway was defended by towers and drawbridges, occupied by a great force of the most daring men in the English army, recently returned from victories in Gascony, Guienne and Poictou. The King of France looked on this densely armed position with despair, and after vainly challenging King Edward to come out and fight in the open, he withdrew.

The starving people of Calais, who, on seeing the approach of the huge French army had hung out their banners on the walls, lighted bonfires, and rejoiced at their coming salvation, were now plunged into the darkest misery. They lowered all their banners except the great flag of France which floated on the loftiest tower. But the next day, in their utter dejection, they pulled it down and ran up the banner of England in token of surrender. It was 4 August 1347.

With his people starving, the governor asked Edward for the lives and liberties of the citizens as the sole condition of surrender, but Edward being incensed at their obstinate resistance was determined to punish them all for it. However, appeals to his chivalry from his own officers softened his resolve and he compromised his anger by demanding that six of the leading citizens should be sacrificed instead of the whole people, and that the ill-fated six should come to his camp in their shirts, bareheaded and barefooted, with halters round their necks, and bearing the keys of the city.

Six prominent citizens volunteered their lives to save the others and went to Edward in the condition he had demanded. The king ordered them to instant execution, but his queen begged for their lives and he could not refuse her.

Heavy cannons blasting a fortified city in the early 15th century.

With the increased use of gunpowder and cannons, the former was used in the mines instead of brushwood and bacon fat, with more devastating effect, and heavy artillery replaced the antiquated missile-throwing engines. English guns helped capture the French town of Harfleur in 1415 and smashed the walls of Le Mans in a couple of days in 1424. Bamburgh Castle in Northumberland is believed to have been the first fortress on English soil to be subdued by cannon fire, in 1464 during the Wars of the Roses.

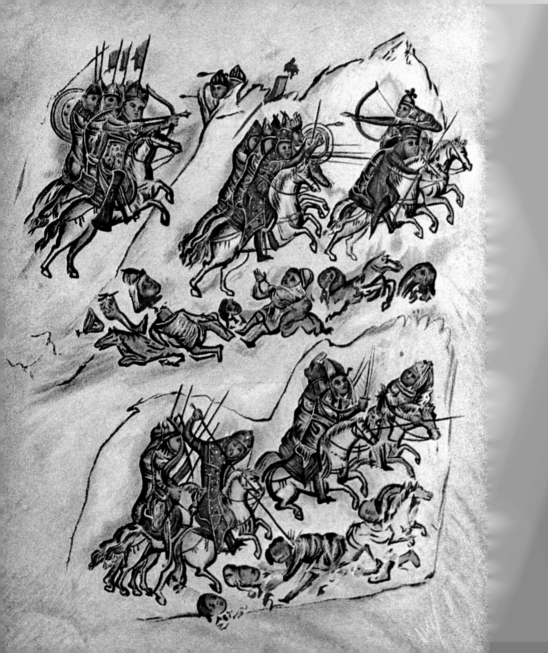

Bellum ibi Gwido de Turri euasit.

Chapter Eight

THE BARONS' WAR

EDWARD I OF England was a warrior king who enjoyed great military success. A brilliant general, he displayed a grasp of tactics and strategy unusual in the Middle Ages. During his father's reign (Henry III) he defeated the powerful Simon de Montfort to end the Barons' War, and later fought in the Crusades; as king he conquered Wales and Scotland.

The beau idéal of a medieval knight, Edward was known as 'Longshanks' for he was much taller than most men of his time; broad-shouldered, energetic, and superbly courageous in battle, he was famed for his feats in jousting, hunting, falconry and wrestling. It is said he spoke with a lisp but this did not impair the vigour of his speech. Mostly chivalrous, he loved and respected his father and mother and could forgive his foes. 'No man', he said, 'ever asked mercy of me and was refused.'

The Barons' War came about over the misgovernment of Henry III, a man 'with a heart of wax' who could not keep his promises or pay his debts. In 1258 the principal barons of England, headed by the formidable Simon de Montfort, Earl of Leicester, forced Henry to agree to a plan of reform, called 'the Provisions of Oxford', which restricted royal power by placing the

Edward I of England, a warrior king of considerable tactical skill, an unusual attribute in the Middle Ages.

Simon de Montfort, formidable leader of the barons'
revolt against Henry III.
Illustration based on the
window in Chartres Cath-
edral, *c.* 1231.

administration in the hands of twenty-four barons. A few years later Henry
repudiated the agreement and sought to regain his authority, an action which
resulted in the barons taking up arms against him.

In the civil war that ensued, the northern counties and those along the
Welsh borders declared for the king, while the Midlands, the Cinque Ports,
and London supported de Montfort. Earl Simon, son of a noted Crusader,
endeavoured to impart a sacred character to his cause by recounting to his
soldiers the many perjuries of the king, 'who had broken so many oaths that
he had become the enemy of God', and induced them to wear white crosses
on their surcoats.

The rival armies met in the battle of Lewes, in Sussex, on 14 May 1264.
The royalists were divided into three divisions: King Henry commanded
the centre body, his brother Richard, Earl of Cornwall, the body on the
left, and Prince Edward (then twenty-five years old) the body on the right.
The baronial army was formed in five divisions, with de Montfort leading

King Henry in danger in the battle of Evesham, 1265. Prince Edward is shown dashing to his father's aid.

the third; the fourth division, headed by Nicholas Seagrave, consisted entirely of Londoners.

The exact strengths of the armies are unknown, but the king's force was the larger, stiffened with many foreign crossbowmen and veteran soldiers. The other side was largely made up of new recruits and raw levies.

The knight of this period wore mail armour from head to foot, with additional solid armour plates protecting his knees. Over his suit of mail he wore a loose, sleeveless, brightly coloured linen surcoat. A close-fitting mail coif covered his head and neck, leaving only his face exposed; over the coif he wore either a flat-topped, barrel-shaped helm or the newer type of conical helm that provided a glancing surface to deflect weapon blows. The helm often sported a crest bearing the knight's heraldic device.

Secured to his shoulders by straps he wore curious protective plates called 'ailettes', made of steel or hardened leather, which sloped from his helmet to his shoulder points. These ailettes were shaped in rectangles, diamonds or discs and also bore the owner's heraldic device. The knightly shield of the time was small, traditional in shape, made of wood covered with leather and decorated with heraldic designs. The horseman fought with lance, sword, axe, mace, and a short stabbing dagger for desperate action at close quarters.

Superior foot-soldiers wore the mail hauberk, or shirt, covered by a surcoat. They battled with polearms, sword and buckler, the latter being a small round shield. Their helmets were the iron kettle shape or skullcaps. Archers used the longbow and the crossbow. The untrained peasant levies had no armour and used a variety of primitive weapons, including farming implements such as the scythe, and the hand-sling for hurling stones. The brunt of the fighting was done by the heavy horsemen with the infantry in support.

On the morning of the battle of Lewes, de Montfort left his camp and marched against the enemy; he seized the heights above the town and forced the royalists to attack. Earl Simon had taken the precaution of holding a reserve in readiness. King Henry, confident of victory, had not troubled himself with any planning. His proud knights, champing at the bit, eager to get at the enemy, would win him the day.

The fight opened with Prince Edward leading his knights and men-at-arms in a spirited charge against the Londoners. Unskilled in war, the London citizens quickly gave way before the heavy horsemen and turned and fled in panic. Burning to avenge the insults previously heaped on his mother by the Londoners (who had emptied filth upon the queen and threatened to drown her for a witch), Edward pursued them relentlessly over four miles without giving quarter to a single man until 5,000 bodies littered the way.

In taking this reckless action, Edward had left the royal army weakened and vulnerable. Meanwhile, the experienced de Montfort rapidly exploited the prince's absence. He marshalled his forces, brought up his fresh reserve, and led them in a compact mass against the main division commanded by the king. Crowded in a narrow space, with a river in their rear, the royalist centre and left were crushed and Henry and his chief nobles were taken prisoner. When the impetuous prince returned from his vengeful pursuit the battle was already lost and he was captured by a body of horsemen.

Victory at Lewes placed Simon de Montfort at the head of the State. He released the king but kept Prince Edward as a hostage. Earl Simon brought about a significant change in the Great Council or Parliament. Hitherto the Great Council had consisted only of the nobility and clergy, who held land direct from the king, and were called together by him to give money and advice. When de Montfort called a meeting in 1265 he summoned not only the barons and bishops who had always attended, but also two knights from each shire and two townsmen from each of those cities and boroughs which could be depended upon to support his reforms. This is often referred to as the first Parliament because it was the first in which the 'Commons' were represented.

Dissensions split the baronial party. Perhaps de Montfort's arrogance had a lot to do with it. The Earl of Gloucester went over to the royalists, enabled Prince Edward to escape from captivity, and joined him with other barons in raising an army to fight de Montfort. Edward had learned a salutary lesson at Lewes and his handling of the campaign of Evesham in July and August 1265 was masterly.

Earl Simon's eldest son, also named Simon, was besieging a royalist stronghold in Sussex while his father was fighting in Wales. Earl Simon now endeavoured to join forces with his son – a measure that Edward did his best to prevent by taking possession of the fords of the Severn and destroying the boats and bridges on that river, thereby keeping Simon the elder in Wales. By a circuitous route, young Simon marched to join his father and Edward found himself in the middle of the two armies, whose combined strength far outnumbered his own.

To avoid being caught in the pincer and to prevent the union of the enemy forces, Edward decided to attack the young Simon. Leaving the Severn,

Simon de Montfort's last stand at Evesham. After he was killed, Earl Simon's head was cut off and paraded on a lance.

Edward made a forced march through the night and launched a surprise dawn attack on the enemy camp near Kenilworth, in Warwickshire, and virtually wiped out the soldiers. Simon managed to escape to nearby Kenilworth Castle, a de Montfort stronghold.

Edward immediately marched back to Worcester to prevent Earl Simon crossing the Severn, but too late, de Montfort had crossed into England and was proceeding to Kenilworth by way of Evesham to join his son, unaware of his total defeat. Edward divided his army into three divisions, with orders to converge with all haste on Evesham. Once again he force-marched his weary men through the night and on 4 August had de Montfort's small army trapped within a loop of the River Avon. While two of Edward's divisions closed the open side of the pocket, the third force stood on the far bank at the rear, cutting off a retreat across the river.

Observing Edward's skilful deployment, Earl Simon commented, 'They

Prince Edward defeats Sir
Adam Gourdon in single
combat. The prince spared
his life and treated him well.

come on wisely, but it was from me they learned it.' With his 7,000 men, mostly untrained Welsh levies armed with billhooks and scythes, surrounded by 20,000 superior soldiers, de Montfort said quietly, 'May God have mercy on our souls, for our bodies are Prince Edward's.'

Nevertheless, like the great warrior he was, Earl Simon prepared to fight to the end. Having spent a short time in prayer and taken the sacrament, as was his custom before entering battle, he formed his men in compact order and placed himself at their head. He attempted a desperate charge to force a way through the royalists but was unsuccessful. He then rallied his men in a solid mass on the summit of a hill and was closely surrounded by the enemy.

King Henry, still the earl's prisoner, was clad in mail and sat on a horse. During the confusion of the fight he was thrown from his mount and only escaped being killed by his own side by calling out, 'Stay your hand, I am Harry of Winchester' (so-called from the place of his birth). Prince Edward came to his father's assistance and took him to a place of safety.

Several times the royalists attacked the valiant little group on the hill and were repulsed with heavy losses. De Montfort was unhorsed but continued fighting on foot. His son Henry was killed at his side. At length the redoubtable earl himself, after surviving most of the champions of his cause, and standing almost alone was cut down with his sword in hand. Chivalry was forgotten that savage day. The royalists gave no quarter to rich or poor; no offer of ransom stayed the uplifted arms of the victors. The bodies of de Montfort and his son were brutally mutilated and the earl's head paraded on a lance.

King Henry was restored to power, but he was little more than a cipher, Prince Edward being the real ruler of England. The barons' revolt, however, was not entirely over. Simon de Montfort the younger, with a small force of men, still survived in the isles of Axholme and Ely, while his retainers continued to hold the castle of Kenilworth against repeated assaults. The Cinque Ports maintained an obstinate defence, and in the forest of Hampshire the famous Sir Adam Gourdon defied the royal authority.

Gourdon was one of the most gallant knights of his time and from the recesses of the forest he conducted rapid raids against the royal troops, inflicting severe losses. Prince Edward took the field against the rebels but in two years failed to bring them to submission. Finally, by the agreement called the *Dictum de Kenilworth* the rebel barons were granted an amnesty and regained their forfeited estates by the payment of a fine.

A chivalrous act on the part of Prince Edward, in battle with Sir Adam

Gourdon, helped greatly to extinguish the spirit of disaffection. The prince engaged Gourdon in single combat and unhorsed him. With the vanquished knight at his mercy, Edward spared his life, entertained him and obtained for him a full pardon, taking 'Sir Adam into his special favour, and was ever afterwards faithfully served by him'.

With England restored to a state of peace, Edward took the cross and went on a Crusade to the Holy Land in 1270. He came to the throne in 1272 on the death of Henry and later conquered Wales and Scotland.

Chapter Nine   LONGBOW AND CROSSBOW

ONGBOWS, in the strong hands of trained English archers, were fast-shooting, far-reaching weapons of tremendous impact and importance. Employed *en masse*, the longbow was capable of destroying a charge by mounted knights; the dark clouds of droning arrows 'falling thick as snow' pierced armoured riders and horses with a hard clout that transformed a spirited rush into a wretched rout. A simple weapon wielded by yeomen of humble birth, the longbow laid low the finest French chivalry at Crécy, Poitiers, and Agincourt during the Hundred Years War. Expert use of the weapon elevated the English army to one of the most successful in western Europe in the fourteenth and fifteenth centuries.

Peculiar to the English (the French and others favoured the crossbow), the longbow was ideally suited to the Englishman's sturdy physique. A foreign visitor of the time commented that the bows were 'thicker and longer than those used by other nations, just as the Englishmen are stronger than other people'. Mastery of the longbow depended not on strength of arm alone but of the whole body. Its exponents were trained from youth, taught to lay their bodies to the bow, progressing to weapons of increasing size as

English longbowman of the
Hundred Years War.

they grew bigger and stronger. A full size longbow, some six feet in length, required a pull of from 80lb to over 100lb draw weight and the archer matured into a muscular figure capable of sustained shooting for several minutes at a time.

The English preferred their bowstaves to be made from well-seasoned yew but elm, ash, and beech were also employed to prevent the total destruction of yew trees. The 'bowyer', the maker of the bowstaves, became a privileged craftsman in the land, as did the 'fletcher' who feathered the arrows. The bowyer fashioned the six feet of rough wood into a curve of beauty with a two-inch diameter in the middle, tapering gradually to narrow ends fitted with horn tips, the latter notched to secure the bowstring of hemp or flax, which was regularly rubbed with beeswax to prevent fraying.

The arrows, three feet long, were made from many kinds of woods, in particular yew, Brazil, birch, elm, and aspen; they were fitted with steel 'piles' or points of various shapes and sizes. The narrow bodkin head, for example, was used for penetrating armour at 250 yards range; the crescent-shaped head was used to hamstring horses or to cut the rigging of ships. The fletcher (from the French *flèche* for arrow) fitted each shaft with three feathers, goose feathers being the favoured choice but swan, turkey, and peacock fletchings were also used.

> *No roaring guns were then in use*
> *They dreamt of no such thing*
> *Our Englishmen in fight did use*
> *The gallant grey-goose wing.*
> *And with the gallant grey-goose wing*
> *Against the French did win the day*
> *They made their horses kick and fling*
> *And down their riders lay.*

The English archer of the Hundred Years War was a true professional fighting man, he took great care of his weapons and cropped his hair short so that it would not blow in his eyes to disturb his aim. He marched into battle with a sheaf (twenty-four) of arrows held in a bundle by a loop from his belt. He carried his bow unstrung in a case, his bowstrings and beeswax in a pouch. In action he stood in a steady position, his arrows stuck in the ground beside him, ready for rapid use; when these were gone young lads fetched more from the arrow wagon.

Each bowman frequently carried a stake six feet long sharpened at both ends so that in battle they fixed the stakes in the ground at an angle to form a *chevaux de frise* against enemy cavalry, and with their flanks secure they could hold their ground even against steel-clad chivalry. For close-quarter combat the archer carried a sword, battle-axe, and a maul or mallet.

As regards protective clothing, he wore whatever he could take from enemy dead or prisoners, including various pieces of armour and helmets. A popular item of bowman's apparel was the brigadine jacket, a sleeveless leather tunic lined with iron plates which allowed free movement of the arms. Monstrelet in his chronicles describes the English bowmen at Agincourt (1415) as being for the most part without armour and in jackets, without hats or caps and often barefooted (to give surer purchase on the ground). Their axes or swords hung at their girdles. St Remy says that many wore caps of *cuir bouilli* (boiled leather) and others of wickerwork crossed over with bars of iron.

The great advantage the longbow enjoyed over the crossbow was in rapid shooting: six or more arrows could be discharged in the time it took a crossbowman to shoot one bolt. An old time historian stated that 'A first rate English archer who in a single minute was unable to draw and discharge his bow twelve times, with a range of 250 yards, and who in these twelve shots once missed his man, was very lightly esteemed.'

The longbowman pulled back his string to his ear (as opposed to the chest or chin with the shortbow); the first three fingers of his right hand were protected by a leather guard, his left wrist was encased in a horn bracer as a

A longbowman and a spear-
man of north Wales depicted
in a drawing of the 13th
century. Strangely enough
the longbow shown here
appears to be more of a
shortbow. The reason for one
bare foot is to ensure better
purchase on the ground.

shield against the bowstring's whip. The longbow had a range of 350 to 400
yards, its steel-tipped arrows could easily pierce armour at 250 yards.
Gerald de Barri, the twelfth-century Welsh cleric-historian, recorded that
longbow arrows had penetrated an oak door four fingers thick, their points
protruding on the other side. Which brings us to the Welsh origin of the
longbow.

The southern Welsh were the first exponents of the longbow, the people
of Gwent (Monmouth and Glamorgan) being acknowledged as the best.
The northern Welsh were not archers, but spearmen. Edward I, that outstanding warrior king of England, introduced the longbow into his army
after being impressed by the weapon during his conquest of Wales, 1282–84.
Although the English became masters of the longbow, contingents of Welsh
archers served in the English army during the Hundred Years War.

In the battle of Falkirk, 1298, Edward I employed a large number of
Welsh bowmen against the Scots, under William Wallace. Falkirk was the
first battle of importance in which longbowmen played a key role. The
Scottish army consisted mainly of spearmen armed with long pikes. Wallace
formed his 25,000 spearmen in four great hollow circles, or 'schiltrons'
(round phalanxes), with the outer ranks kneeling. Archers armed with the
shortbow were placed between the schiltrons, and the cavalry were drawn
up as a reserve in the rear.

When Edward's mounted vanguard failed to break the walls of pikes, he
brought his longbowmen to the front, who proceeded to decimate the
Scottish schiltrons with a thunderstorm of arrows. Having thoroughly

English yeomen at the butts, c. 1340. Archery practice was made compulsory throughout the land. Illustration from the Loutrell Psalter.

weakened and demoralized the pikemen, Edward launched his cavalry to finish the task. This victory established the value of the longbow and the successful combination of archers supported by heavy horsemen which served the English well in future battles. Robert Bruce managed to score a rare Scots triumph at Bannockburn in 1314 by scattering the English archers with his cavalry at the start of the fight; it must be said however that the English were badly led that day by Edward II.

By the time Edward III came to the throne in 1327 the longbow had become the English weapon *par excellence*. He conferred honour on the longbow by raising a corps of archers of the King's Guard, consisting of 120 men, the most expert in the kingdom. Archery practice became compulsory and throughout the land young lads at the village butts developed strong bodies and keen eyes in bending the bow in training and in competition. In 1363 and again in 1388 statutes were passed calling upon the people to put aside their popular amusements and to practise archery instead: 'Servants and labourers shall have bows and arrows, and use the same on Sundays and holidays, and leave all playing at tennis or football, and other games called coits, dice, casting the stone, kailes, and other such inopportune games.'

Archers made up a considerable part of the English army; they were proud, disciplined, well-paid professionals who most certainly earned their money and fame by whipping the French armoured *noblesse* at Crécy, Poitiers, and Agincourt. A splendid weapon though it was in speed, accuracy and economy, the longbow had the singular disadvantage of requiring practised skill to handle it effectively, 'for men shall never shoot well unless they be brought up to it'. And this constant demand for expertise led to its gradual abandonment in favour of the handgun and long pike.

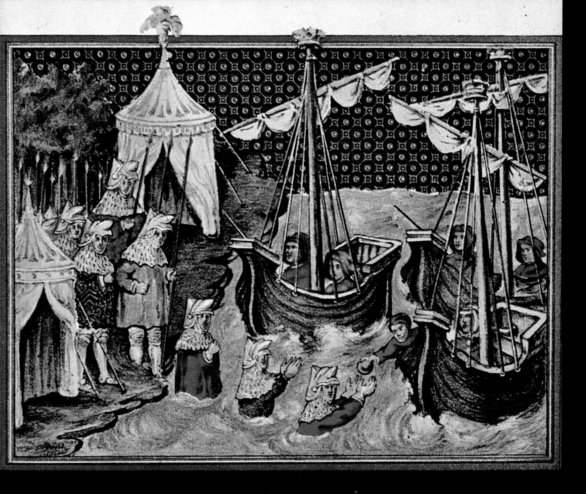

Bringing provisions to Richard II's army in Ireland.

The duel on London Bridge in 1390 between Scottish knight
Sir David de Lindsay and English knight John, Lord Welles.

In marked contrast the crossbow, or 'arbalest' required little strength and training of its operatives and was much favoured by the French, Italians, Germans and others. The Genoese in particular were renowned as mercenary crossbowmen. Although outclassed in rapid shooting by the longbow, the arbalest was a formidable weapon, efficient, accurate, hard-hitting, with a range of up to 400 yards. Of ancient origin, the crossbow rose to prominence in Europe in the twelfth century (its first recorded appearance in western warfare being in the battle of Hastings, 1066, when the Normans used both the arbalest and the shortbow).

The arrow shot by the crossbow was called a 'bolt' or 'quarrel'; it was shorter and stouter than a longbow shaft, with a heavier head, and was 'fletched' with leather or thin wooden flights. These bolts inflicted such dreadful wounds that a Lateran Council of 1139 prohibited the use of the 'treacherous, murderous' crossbow amongst Christian nations, but allowed its use against infidels. Nevertheless, it was too good a weapon to ignore and despite the papal ban it was widely used in internecine Christian wars.

Richard I of England (1189–1199) employed crossbowmen in his army when fighting Philip Augustus of France. Richard died from a wound by an arbalest bolt. Philip Augustus (1180–1233) organized bodies of foot and mounted arbalesters; these regiments became so important that their commander was given the title of Grand Master of Crossbowmen, a high post

English longbowman and man-at-arms at the time of Agincourt, 1415. The bowmen stuck their arrows in the ground ready for rapid shooting.

English archers of the 16th century, also armed with sword and buckler, the latter a small round shield for close combat.

in the French army, and it was not till 1515 that this office was united with that of Grand Master of Artillery. Edward I of England hired expensive Gascon arbalesters for his early Welsh campaigns until enamoured by the virtues of the cheap, fast-shooting Welsh longbow; in 1282 Edward fielded 850 crossbowmen, by 1289 this had fallen to 105 and in 1292 to a mere 70. However, on the Continent the crossbow remained a popular weapon throughout the fourteenth and fifteenth centuries.

The arbalest consisted of a short, powerfully sprung wooden or composite bow mounted at right angles on a straight wooden stock; later bows were made of steel leaves. The thick bowstring was pulled back and held in the spanned or 'cocked' position by a latch or nut triggered by a lever under the stock. The bolt was placed in a groove, in front of the bowstring, on top of the stock. The operative raised the weapon to his cheek, took aim, and discharged the missile by raising the lever, which released the bowstring.

Early crossbows could be spanned by hand, with some effort, but as the bows grew more powerful and stiff, mechanical devices had to be employed. In the thirteenth century the crossbow was spanned by the aid of a hook attached to the arbalester's waist belt; he placed his foot in the stirrup fixed to the front of the weapon, then stooped to engage the bowstring in the hook hanging from his belt, by straightening himself, using the whole force

A Genoese crossbowman spanning his bow with a windlass.

Here we see the spanning, loading, and shooting of the crossbow.

of his body, he could span the bow and catch the string on the retaining nut, ready for shooting. Crossbows of the fifteenth century were spanned by a windlass, or 'cranequin', which wound the string into place with little expenditure of strength, albeit a slow operation.

In open battle the arbalester often used a large, rectangular shield called a 'pavise' or 'mantlet', about five feet high, which he propped up to provide cover while he spanned his weapon. Crossbows were particularly effective in defending the walls of a castle or city under siege, where the rate of fire at a single loophole could be doubled by stationing two arbalesters at the same post, one shooting while the other reloaded. The crossbow was finally ousted by reliable handguns in the sixteenth century.

Chapter Ten

THE HUNDRED YEARS WAR

THE LONG series of campaigns, truces and periods of peace between England and France which lasted from 1337 to 1453 are known collectively as the Hundred Years War, although they actually spanned 120 years. The fighting took place in France and we shall concern ourselves mainly with three major land battles: Crécy 1346, Poitiers 1356, and Agincourt 1415.

The war had its origin in the disputes over French lands held in fief by the English crown; the aid given by the French to the Scots in their wars against England; and the interference by the French in the profitable wool trade between the English merchants and the Flemish cities. Also, Edward III of England claimed the French throne by right of his mother Isabella, daughter of the French king Philip IV.

The first action of importance was the English naval victory in the Flemish port of Sluys in June 1340, when Edward III with some 150 vessels destroyed the French fleet of about 190 ships. The battle commenced at ten in the morning and lasted nine hours. Genoese crossbowmen in the service of France showered the king's ships with their bolts, but were briskly answered by the quick-shooting longbows of the English.

When all the arrows were spent, the ships closed with grappling irons and chains and the men-at-arms boarded and fought with swords and axes, as if on land. The English took or destroyed nearly the whole of the enemy fleet. Thousands of Frenchmen were drowned. So great was the defeat that no one dared tell Philip VI; it was only made known to him by the court jester. 'Oh, the cowardly English!' exclaimed the fool. 'Why so?' asked the king. 'Because', replied the jester, 'at Sluys the other day they had not the courage to jump into the sea, as did our noble Frenchmen.'

Edward landed in Flanders and besieged Tournai, but later abandoned the siege and made a truce with Philip. After six years of alternate war and truce came the significant battle of Crécy on 26 August 1346. Edward invaded Normandy with an army of some 25,000 men composed of knights, mounted and armoured men-at-arms, Welsh and Irish infantry, and a powerful force of English archers armed with the longbow. The king was accompanied by his eldest son Edward, Prince of Wales, a lad of sixteen, whom historians later dubbed the Black Prince by the colour of his armour.

It is interesting to note that during this campaign a knight was paid two shillings a day, a man-at-arms a shilling a day, a mounted archer sixpence a day, a foot-archer threepence a day, and the humble foot-soldier twopence a day. 'Bannerets' – veteran knights of proved valour who directed contingents in the field and served as staff officers to the commanders, were paid four shillings a day.

In comparison, a master carpenter in England received threepence a day, and a reaper twopence. Land could be rented at fourpence an acre a year. Soldiers on campaign had the opportunity to enrich themselves by plunder and the ransom of wealthy prisoners.

Edward marched inland, captured Caen and ravaged the countryside. Philip raised a large army of 60,000 and moved to meet the English. Edward chose a battleground near the village of Crécy-en-Ponthieu, near Abbeville, and deployed his forces with care and skill on a low rise sloping gently to the south-east, with a windmill on its summit from which he could overlook the whole field of battle.

The English now numbered, owing to previous losses, about 13,000 strong, half of them archers. Edward divided his army into three divisions or 'battles'. He placed one on the right under the Earls of Warwick and Oxford with the Prince of Wales as titular commander, and one on the left under the Earls of Arundel and Northampton. The third 'battle', standing back some distance from the others, was held in reserve under the personal command of the king.

The nucleus of each division was a phalanx of dismounted men-at-arms (horses and baggage train were placed well in the rear). Each division was flanked by archers and some small bombards which 'threw little iron balls to frighten the horses' – the first use of artillery in field warfare. As a further protection the English had dug numerous small pot-holes in front of their position to trap and upset the enemy horsemen.

Plate armour was now replacing mail armour and a knight wore a breast plate, arm and leg plates, and a heavy helmet complete with a visor that

The battle of Crécy as depicted in an illuminated MS. of the period.

The battle of Poitiers, 19 September 1356. Mounted French knights crash into the stalwart ranks of English archers and men-at-arms.

covered his face in combat. He wore a short surcoat emblazoned with his armorial device, and fought with a lance (couched under his arm), a long sword and a mace. Archers were protected by a mixture of mail shirts, jerkins of toughened leather, and steel caps; in addition to their bows and arrows they carried swords, axes, and knives for close-quarter fighting.

In marked contrast to Edward's thoughtful preparation, Philip's huge army blundered into battle without any attention to tactical organization. Eager to get at the English, the French had marched in great haste, confident they would sweep the enemy from the field. Philip's force was composed of some 12,000 heavy cavalry, 17,000 light cavalry, 6,000 mercenary Genoese crossbowmen, and 25,000 peasant levies. Riding with the heavy horse, the flower of French chivalry, were the kings of Bohemia and Majorca.

On reaching the battleground, Philip attempted to halt his ponderous army for deployment. The vanguard of the juggernaut pulled up but those following continued to press forward and massed confusion ensued. Each knightly lord wanted his share of glory in the front and was not disposed to obey orders. During this time a thunderstorm burst over the field. When it cleared shortly after, the sun shone brightly into the Frenchmen's eyes and on the backs of the English.

Philip ordered his crossbowmen to the front to open the battle. But they complained they were unready for combat; the long march had wearied them and the sudden downpour had soaked and rendered slack their bow-strings. On hearing this complaint the Count of Alençon, Philip's brother, commented sourly: 'This is what we get by employing scoundrels who fail us when most we need them.'

This pricked the Genoese into action. Jean Froissart, the fourteenth-century French historian, records:

'The Genoese set up a loud shout in order to frighten them, but the English remained quite still. They set up a second shout and advanced a little forward, but the English never moved. They shouted a third time, advancing with their crossbows presented, and began to shoot [but their bolts, launched by slack strings, fell short]. The English archers then advanced one step forward [in order to pull back their strings, which they had kept dry] and shot their arrows with such force and quickness that it seemed as if it snowed. When the Genoese felt these arrows pierce their arms, heads, and through their armour, they flung down their crossbows and ran back.'

Angered by the fleeing Genoese, Philip commanded his forward knights to 'Kill me those runaway rascals for they stop our path without reason!'

Obediently the glittering horsemen dashed into the ill-fated mercenaries and slaughtered a great many. The French chivalry held all foot-soldiers in utter contempt and regarded them as unnecessary on the field of battle; in their code of war only the knights counted.

The French horse charged on towards the English, who continued to shoot arrows thick and fast, bringing down knights in large numbers. More French horsemen barged their way forward from the main body into the devastating hail of shafts. As the knights tumbled heavily to the ground, Welsh and Irish foot-soldiers armed with daggers slipped out of the English ranks and killed the horsemen as they lay stunned or wounded.

Some knights managed to survive the hail of arrows and reach the division of the Prince of Wales, who found himself hard pressed. A messenger galloped to King Edward to request assistance for the young prince, but the king refused to send help, saying, 'Let the boy win his spurs, for I am determined, if it pleases God, that the glory and honour of this day shall be his.'

On the French side an incident of foolhardy chivalry concerned the near-blind and aged King of Bohemia. 'I pray you', he cried to his knight attendants, 'to lead me into the thick of the fight that I may strike one good blow with this old sword of mine.' Accordingly, the two knights secured their reins to those of the king's horse and thus linked together all three rushed into the midst of the battle, and all were killed.

After sixteen futile charges the battered French finally quitted the field at night in complete disorder. Edward forbade his men to pursue and they remained in ranks guarding their position until dawn. The Prince of Wales won his spurs right enough. The great victory, however, had been won by the resolute bowmen of England. The defeat stunned the French people, the very best of their chivalry had been wiped out by humble archers; mounted knights had been slaughtered by common foot-soldiers! It was military (and social) heresy.

The French losses were enormous: more than 1,500 lords and knights and some 30,000 other ranks. English casualties were extremely light, about 200 dead, including two knights. Crécy demolished the dictum that cavalry were the dominant, decisive factor on the battlefield. It had been clearly demonstrated that dismounted troops supported by archers, if properly managed and deployed, could defeat heavy horsemen with simple economy. From the day of Crécy Feudalism, of which the mounted knight was the linchpin, tottered slowly but surely to its grave.

John II, King of France, commanded his army at Poitiers and fought bravely.

King John and his son, Prince Philip, hard-pressed at Poitiers.

Surprisingly enough, the French learned very little from the terrible lesson of Crécy. The nobles persisted in the blinkered belief that they had been vanquished by the English knights and men-at-arms. From 1347 to 1354 England and France observed a truce, both nations being devastated by the pestilence called the 'Black Death', which swept over Europe carrying off more than a third of the population.

The war was resumed in 1355 when Edward, Prince of Wales raided deep into southern France and returned to Bordeaux laden with the booty of hundreds of cities, towns and villages. In the following year he plundered his way through central France. On 17 September, near the city of Poitiers, he ran into a French army far larger than his own, commanded by John II.

The two sides prepared for battle. Edward chose an excellent position for a defensive stand, on elevated ground with his flanks protected by vineyard walls and trenches, to which there was but one approach, a long deep lane between hedgerows, so narrow that only four horsemen could ride through it abreast. Behind these hedgerows were placed strong bodies of archers. At

King John surrenders to the Prince of Wales, his cousin, on the field of Poitiers, by handing him his right gauntlet.

the end of the lane, behind a thick hedge, Edward deployed his dismounted knights and men-at-arms in three battles, similar in position to that used at Crécy, with archers on the flanks.

The English army numbered about 12,000 of which some 8,000 were cavalry and 3,000 archers. The French force totalled about 35,000, including 16,000 horsemen and 2,000 crossbowmen. With such an advantage in men the French were sure of victory and keen to join battle. The humiliation of Crécy had yet to be avenged. In commonsense military terms there was no need for the battle. The English had virtually no provisions, some had not eaten for days, and King John could have played the waiting game and starved them into submission. But there was little martial glory in that mundane method.

Before the fight commenced, at midday on 19 September, Edward had tried to negotiate a peaceful settlement with John, offering to give up all his plunder and prisoners, and to pledge himself not to bear arms against France for seven years, in exchange for a free withdrawal for his hungry, outnumbered army. John refused the offer, demanding the prince's unconditional surrender. Edward declined and resolved to fight.

Recalling that the English cavalry had triumphed on foot at Crécy, John dismounted most of his horsemen, who cut down their twenty-foot lances to six foot. He deployed his dismounted knights and men-at-arms in three huge divisions, placed one after the other, with two units of cavalry in front. He decided to launch a frontal attack through the narrow lane, wave after wave without any regard to tactics or manoeuvre. He failed to see the great disadvantage that dismounted knights would have in attacking a strong position defended by foot-soldiers.

The battle opened with a charge of 300 French horse. The English bowmen behind the hedges slaughtered the gleaming chivalry with ease at short range, their flashing barbs piercing armour and horse. Next came the marching battle commanded by the Dauphin. Despite ghastly losses inflicted by the bowmen, the French managed to press forward and engage the dismounted English knights in fierce combat. But the French, unaccustomed to fighting without their horses, soon began to tire and were driven back. However, the English had been badly mauled.

The awful sight of the Dauphin's shattered division, dispelled the fighting spirit of the second division, commanded by the Duke of Orléans, which retreated in confusion before coming into range of the terrible rain of English arrows. The climax of the carnage came with John, a warrior king

Bertrand du Guesclin, one of the outstanding soldiers of the Hundred Years War, became Constable of France, the highest military rank.

Du Guesclin's men mount a surprise attack on an English supply train.

not easily intimidated, leading the final assault of the largest division of dismounted men, which appeared as numerous as the entire English army.

The French were exhausted by marching a mile in their stifling armour. The English were also weary after prolonged fighting. Fearing that his soldiers could not withstand another determined attack, Edward decided to commit his reserve of 400 mounted knights to a charge, taking the added precaution of sending a body of horsemen and archers to hit the French in the rear.

With a cry of 'Advance, banners, in the name of God and St George!' Edward led the gallop. The horsemen collided with John's division with such great impact that legend has it the crash was heard in Poitiers, seven miles away. As the two forces slashed, hacked and stabbed in blind fury, Edward's other contingent struck the French from behind. The Frenchmen wavered and began to quit the field. King John, with a hard core of nobles, continued to fight on with his battle axe; Prince Philip stood by his side, warning him of danger: 'Father, guard yourself on the right – guard yourself on the left!'

There was fierce competition amongst the English surrounding the king to capture him for his enormous ransom value. 'Surrender, sire, or you are a dead man!' But John fought on, unwilling to yield to anyone of inferior rank. Froissart gives an account of his surrender:

'The king, being hard pressed, repeatedly asked, "Where is my cousin? Where is the Prince of Wales?" Then said a young knight, in French, "Sire, he is not here, but surrender yourself to me and I will lead you to him." Struck by the pure accent, the king asked, "Who are you?" The Frenchman replied, "I am Denis de Morbeque, a knight of Artois, but I serve the King of England because I have been banished from France." John then gave him his right-hand gauntlet, saying, "To you I surrender." And he and his son were conducted to the Prince of Wales.'

So ended the battle of Poitiers. Again the French had suffered a traumatic defeat, losing some 25,000 dead, mostly knights and men-at-arms; about the same number were taken prisoner, including many lords and nobles. The English losses were in the region of 2,000 dead and wounded. The Prince of Wales, chivalrous in the extreme, treated his royal captive with great respect. On entering London, John rode a stately white charger, adorned with costly trappings, while Edward rode at his side 'on a little black nag, so studious was he to do honour to his prisoner'.

John remained a captive, enjoying regal comfort and company, in the palace of Savoy until he was released on payment of three million gold crowns at the Peace of Bretigny in 1360. Meanwhile, France was plunged into misery. The routed soldiery of Poitiers turned into free companies of bandits, while the nobles held prisoner by the English purchased their ransom by extortion which drove the peasantry into universal revolt.

By the Peace of Bretigny the King of England waived his claim on the French crown and on the Duchy of Normandy. But he retained the Duchy of Aquitaine – which included Gascony, Guienne, Poictou, and Saintonge – not as a fief but in full sovereignty, while his new conquest of Calais remained a part of the possessions of the English crown.

It is interesting to note the subsequent career of King John, known in history as John the Good. He was in fact a bad king, all his good qualities seemed to belong to the chivalric class. On his return to France he imposed new taxes on the impoverished country, which he justified with promises of reform that he never honoured. He did however see fit to honour another promise. When he learned that his son, who had been left in England as a hostage, had escaped, he redeemed his parole by returning himself to London. A rare instance of fidelity in monarchs, although the chaotic state of affairs in France at the time might have influenced his decision.

According to Froissart, John passed his time in London in 'great rejoicings and recreations, in dinners, suppers, and other sorts of feastings'. But the continuous round of pleasure proved too much for him and he died in London in April 1364, aged forty-five.

Edward Prince of Wales, that flower of English Knighthood, darling of the nation, died of a fever in 1376, aged forty-six. He was buried in Canterbury Cathedral, where his effigy clad in armour rests on his marble tomb, and his crested helm, surcoat, gauntlets, sword and shield can still be seen there. It is said that he gained his sobriquet, the Black Prince, from the colour of his armour and plume, but it might have come from the French calling him *Le Noir* on account of his black deeds in plundering the country. At the time of his death all England's vast territories in France had dwindled to a few towns.

When Charles V came to the French throne on the death of his father, John, he raised the country from the depths of defeat and poverty to renewed wealth and glory. He was called Charles the Wise and wise he was to recognize the genius for war in Bertrand du Guesclin, a rough Breton knight whom he raised to the position of Constable of France, the highest military rank, commander of all the French armies.

Following a period of uneasy peace, Henry V of England renewed his claim to the French crown and resumed the Hundred Years War in 1415. Illustration from a picture in Queen's College, Oxford.

Before the battle of Agincourt, 25 October 1415. Weary French knights wait in position at daybreak ready to engage the English.

Du Guesclin, one of the outstanding soldiers of the Hundred Years War, reconciled chivalry with military commonsense, employing tactics and manoeuvres instead of bull-like charges to the front. In particular he favoured 'unknightly' night attacks, which caused the English to complain of his unchivalrous behaviour. In fighting a guerrilla-type war in an age of rigid, traditional methods, it is not surprising that du Guesclin was very successful.

Born in Brittany in 1314, he was coarse-featured, squat in build, with broad shoulders and muscular arms. 'I am very ugly', he said when a youth. 'I may never please the ladies, but I shall make myself terrible to the enemies of my king.' And indeed he did. After the defeat of Poitiers, while King John was a prisoner, du Guesclin gave much-needed assistance to his eldest son, Charles, who then held the regency. When Charles came to the throne he rewarded du Guesclin for his services.

The tough Breton fought in many battles and was captured several times, but Charles always ransomed his champion and made him Constable of France in 1370. Between them they improved the French military organization, creating new units in a regular army, the establishment of a permanent military staff, and trusted more in drilled foot-soldiers than capricious armoured knights.

Du Guesclin avoided pitched battles with the English, preferring to sap

Mounted French knights engaging dismounted English at Agincourt.

The battle of Agincourt
developed into a desperate
struggle at close-quarters, the
English archers plying sword
and battle-axe with as great
effectiveness as they had done
earlier with the deadly longbow.

their strength and spirit by ambush, skirmish, and by cutting off supplies. He captured English towns and castles until by the end of 1374 all that remained in English hands were Calais, Bordeaux and Bayonne. Du Guesclin died in battle in 1380 while taking the stronghold of Château-neuf-de-Randon. Charles V died in the same year.

Following a period of uneasy peace, the war was resumed by the young Henry V of England, a warrior king who renewed the claim to the French throne. He landed in Normandy with an army of 12,000 in August 1415. After besieging and capturing the town of Harfleur, during which time his army was greatly reduced by battle losses and disease, he marched towards Calais. Near the castle of Agincourt the weakened, hungry English army was confronted by a French force of 30,000 under Charles d'Albret, Constable of France.

The two armies faced each other about a mile apart at opposite ends of freshly ploughed fields between two large woods; the fields being thoroughly sodden by a week of heavy rain. The open frontage between the woods measured about 1,200 yards. Henry adopted a defensive position similar to that employed by the English at Crécy and Poitiers – the dismounted men-at-arms formed into three battles in line abreast, each battle flanked by strong bodies of archers.

Each bowman carried a sharpened stake which he stuck in the ground before him at an angle, in the manner of a *chevaux de frise*, its spike ready to impale enemy horsemen. The English, much wasted by sickness, now numbered about 6,000, of which 5,000 were archers. It is said that Henry, in order to increase the desperation of his brave bowmen, told them that the French had vowed to ruin them forever as archers by cutting off the fingers of all who they captured.

Constable d'Albret had formed his men into three divisions, placed one behind the other; the first two battles were composed of dismounted knights and men-at-arms, the third of horsemen, with crossbowmen placed on the flanks and in between the divisions. This time d'Albret had decided to stand his ground and defend, letting the English attack and destroy themselves, as the French had done at Crécy and Poitiers. For several hours the two armies waited for the other to advance.

Then Henry, realizing what the French commander had in mind, endeavoured to provoke the enemy into impetuous action. He advanced his army for half a mile then halted in the original formation, the archers again planting their sharpened stakes before them. The sight of the hated English so near and so few in number excited the passion of the French chivalry to boiling point and they could not contain themselves. Throwing discipline and caution to the wind, the first division clanked forward, and contingents of mounted knights on the flanks levelled their lances and charged.

The ploughed and sodden fields deprived the armoured gallop of speed and the heavy horsemen moved in slow motion, lurching and sinking in the water-logged ground. In their wake the knights on foot struggled through the sea of mud. The English archers poured their arrows into the close-packed, sluggish enemy and did great slaughter. Of the 1,200 horsemen not more than 120 ever reached the spiked barricade of the bowmen, from which the horses recoiled, throwing their riders to the ground.

Hundreds of wounded, screaming steeds were rushing to and fro, stampeding into the marching division, causing confusion and disorder. Those knights that survived the rain of arrows and reached the English line were cut down by the dismounted men-at-arms and the archers, the latter having a 'savage appearance this day. Many had stripped themselves naked; others

King Henry in combat with the Duke d'Alençon at Agincourt.

had bared their arms and breasts that they might exercise their limbs with more ease and execution.' Besides their bow and arrows, each archer carried a battle axe and sword for close combat. Light and agile, the bowmen sprang upon their heavily encumbered opponents and beat upon their armour 'as though they were smiths hammering upon anvils'.

The French attacked again until they were ruined. The battle lasted about three hours. The French suffered appalling losses. An old chronicler records:

'When some of the enemy's van were slain, those behind pressed over the dead, and others again falling on them, they were immediately put to death; and in three places near Henry's banner so large was a pile of corpses that the English stood on the heaps, which exceeded a man's height, and butchered their adversaries below with their swords and axes.'

Henry himself was always in the thick of the fight and under personal attack; twenty French knights having sworn on the cross of their swords to capture or kill him. Henry presented a provocative, signal target: 'His helmet was of polished steel, surmounted by a crown sparkling with jewels, and his surcoat emblazoned with the Arms of England and France.' At one point he was stunned by a blow from a mace and then confronted by the Duke d'Alençon, who had killed the Duke of York in fighting his way to the king. D'Alençon struck the crown from Henry's head and lifted his sword for a more effectual blow, but the king's attendants cut him down and slew him.

The French lost 5,000 dead, most of them nobles and men-at-arms, and 1,000 were taken prisoner. Constable d'Albret, who cannot be blamed for the defeat brought about by the hasty, impassioned chivalry, was among those killed. English losses have been estimated as low as 'fewer than a hundred' to as high as 1,600; all that can be said with certainty is that they were considerably less than the French casualties. Agincourt was another damaging blow to the ascendancy of the ponderous, imperious, and inefficient armoured knight.

The war continued with further English victories in France until Joan of Arc (Jeanne d'Arc) emerged as a most unusual and successful military leader. A pious peasant girl from the village of Domremy, Joan claimed to have seen holy visions and heard heavenly voices which commanded her to raise the siege of Orléans and conduct Charles, the Dauphin, to Rheims to be crowned. Overcoming the opposition of officials, bishops and nobles, she reached the Dauphin himself and won his belief and support in her sacred mission.

After the battle of Agincourt the victorious English held a thanksgiving service in the field.

Clad in armour, mounted on an armoured charger and bearing the lily banner of France, Joan led an enthusiastic army to the relief of Orléans. Her 'rough soldiers and men-at-arms beheld her with awe, thought her a saint from heaven, left off their swearing and their unholy living and crowded to the altars of the churches on their march.' With Joan as their inspiration, they raised the siege in May 1492. The 'Maid of Orléans' gained victory after victory and on 16 June stood beside the Dauphin in Rheims Cathedral as he was crowned Charles VII.

However, royal support now waned for this remarkable girl and a jealous court intrigued against her. In May 1430 she led a small force to relieve Compiègne, besieged by an English–Burgundian army; she was captured by the Burgundians who delivered her to the vengeful English. Abandoned by Charles, she stood trial for witchcraft and heresy and was condemned to be burned at the stake. She died with great fortitude on 30

May 1431. Joan's brief but influential appearance in the war, when things were going badly for France, inspired a new French nationalism.

The war continued, now almost always to the disadvantage of the English. In July 1453 came the battle of Castillon, in which the English launched an attack of dismounted men-at-arms and pikemen, flanked by archers, against an entrenched position protected by artillery. After their guns had pounded the English to a standstill, the French immediately counter-attacked and swept the enemy from the field. This decisive victory – which stilled the ghosts of Crécy, Poitiers and Agincourt – was followed by the capture of Bordeaux in October 1453, thus bringing to an end the Hundred Years War.

Of all the wide English conquests in France, there remained only the Channel Islands and the seaport of Calais, the latter being taken for France by the Duke of Guise in 1558.

Henry VI was King of England when the Wars of the Roses began.

Chapter Eleven T WARS OF THE ROSES

HE SAGA OF the civil wars that raged over England from 1455 to 1485, the so-called Wars of the Roses, remains a confusion of intrigue, battles, treacheries, murders and executions. The wars resulted from the bitter struggle between the royal houses of York and Lancaster for the crown of England. It is generally believed that the rival forces fought under the emblems of the white rose and the red rose. However, this is not so.

Although the white rose was one of the badges of the York family, the Yorkist armies served under the various banners and badges of the lords and nobles who supported the Yorkist cause. The same applied to the Lancastrian forces; the red rose of Lancaster was not evident until the final battle between the factions. Hubert Cole (see BIBLIOGRAPHY) tells us that the name 'Wars of the Roses' is an eighteenth-century invention.

Essentially a conflict of the nobles, in which the mass of the people took little part, it eventually shattered the feudal system of England. The battles and disasters were limited to the persons immediately engaged in them, the trading and industrial classes were not involved and were little affected by them; the commerce and business of the country went on as before.

Henry VI's queen, Margaret
of Anjou, a strong-willed
Frenchwoman known as the
'She-wolf of France'.

An old French writer, de Comines, says: 'The calamities and misfortunes of the war fall on the soldiers, and especially on the nobility; there are no buildings destroyed or demolished by the war, and the mischief of it falls on those who make war.' The nobles prosecuted the wars for their own interests, and in so doing a great many of them were killed. The long conflict crippled the feudal power of the barons and increased the strength of the growing middle classes.

The *cri de guerre* throughout the fighting was 'Slay the nobles, spare the common soldier.' Men of rank were rarely spared, for dead they could not fight again and their lands could be confiscated by the victors. Thus did the old nobility destroy themselves over a thirty-year period. It has been calculated that the Wars of the Roses cost the lives of two kings, one prince, ten dukes, two marquesses, twenty-one earls, twenty-seven lords, 133 knights, 451 esquires, and 84,998 common soldiers.

During this time the King of England had no standing army. Both the forces of York and Lancaster were raised by a combination of the old feudal system and a new system known as 'livery and maintenance'. Both sides also employed foreign mercenaries who were paid an agreed sum. Under feudal tenure the barons and lords who had been granted estates by the king were obliged to provide a number of soldiers, called a 'retinue', to serve the king in times of war.

By the mid-fifteenth century the feudal type of military service was changing. Because the king had no regular army with which to enforce law and order, the barons maintained small private armies, or household troops to protect their interests. These soldiers (farmers, yeomen, gentry) entered into a contract known as 'livery and maintenance', whereby they agreed to wear the lord's livery and emblem and fight for him when required; in return the *grand seigneur* gave them his protection which, in a land plagued by anarchy, was a great security.

In war, a lord would either bring his private army to serve the king, or pay 'shield money' with which the king could hire mercenaries. The retainers of the Earl of Warwick, known as the 'Kingmaker', wore bright red jackets adorned with his family badge of the 'white bear and ragged staff'. Over their full plate armour the nobles and knights wore a cloth tabard, a short tunic emblazoned with their own heraldic devices; the tabard, the prominent crest on the helmet, and the individual banners distinguished friend from foe in battle. Thus were the Wars of the Roses fought under a confusion of emblems and badges.

The armoured man fought mostly on foot in this period, with sword,
mace, and in particular the long-shafted poleaxe, a weapon favoured by
dismounted knights of the fifteenth century. Archers and 'billmen' (the latter
armed with long-bladed polearms) mostly wore leather 'jacks', or jerkins and
either an iron kettle helmet or a sallet type with neck guard. Although hand-
guns and cannons were used in the Wars of the Roses, the archer still
retained his position of battlefield importance.

When the wars began, Henry VI was King of England. A direct descendant
from John of Gaunt, Duke of Lancaster, a son of Edward III, Henry VI
succeeded in 1422 and reigned for thirty-nine years. Weak and ill in mind and
body, he was subject to bouts of insanity and the reins of government were

taken up by his strong-willed wife Margaret of Anjou, known as the 'she-wolf of France', a woman of great cunning and ferocity in pursuing her aims.

Margaret and her Lancastrian favourites came into conflict with the nobles who supported the leadership of the king's cousin, Richard Plantagenet, Duke of York. In 1454 during Henry's first fit of madness, Richard was elected Protector of England by Parliament. He used his office to imprison the Duke of Somerset, Queen Margaret's chief supporter. However, when Henry recovered his wits and resumed his duties, Margaret persuaded him to dismiss Richard from the government.

With the queen and Somerset restored to power, Richard of York rose in revolt and marched on London with 3,000 men. At his side was his nephew Richard Neville, Earl of Warwick, a major figure in the Wars of the Roses who later became known as the 'Kingmaker'. Henry and Somerset with 2,000 men clashed with the Yorkists in the battle of St Albans in May 1455, and in the fight in the city streets Somerset was killed and the king taken prisoner.

In the first battle of St Albans, 22 May 1455, the fighting took place in the city streets.

Richard of York was killed in the battle of Wakefield in December 1460. When his young son, the Duke of Rutland, begged for mercy he was stabbed to death by the vindictive Lord Clifford.

The excitement proved too much for poor Henry, who had been wounded in the neck by an arrow, and he again lost his reason. Richard of York was made Constable of England, with almost dictatorial power. The intrigue and fighting, with see-saw results, continued over the next five years. In October 1459 Richard was forced to flee to Ireland, and Warwick to Calais, the latter returning to England in the following year.

A prime example of the treachery rampant in the wars was that of Lord Grey de Ruthyn, commander of the Lancastrian vanguard division in the Battle of Northampton, 10 July 1460. King Henry and his chief general, the Duke of Buckingham, had taken up a strong position by the side of the River Nene, the rear and flanks secured by a loop in the river. The entire front of the king's army, some 4,000 strong, being protected by a flooded ditch backed by earthworks and a line of sharpened stakes, behind which were placed cannons.

The Yorkist army of about 20,000 men was led jointly by Lord Warwick and Edward, Earl of March (Richard of York's second son, who later became Edward IV). Although heavy rain had ruined the gunpowder and rendered useless the king's cannon, his entrenched archers brought the Yorkist advance to a standstill before they could storm the ramparts. It is significant that Warwick did not order his own archers to shoot back, for this would have replenished the stock of the enemy bowmen; in the event, the Lancastrians exhausted their arrows.

At this crucial stage, Lord Grey (who had conspired with Warwick before the battle) displayed Warwick's banner of the 'white bear and ragged staff' and commanded his men of the vanguard, on the right of the king's position, to put down their arms and give the advancing Yorkists a hand over the ramparts, which they did. The armoured fighters poured through the breach, by-passed the Lancastrian archers in the centre position and, joined by Lord Grey's turncoats, charged the rear of the king's division on the left.

The battle was now quickly concluded, with the Lancastrians breaking and fleeing across the river, many of them drowning in their cumbersome armour. Buckingham and several other prominent nobles were killed and King Henry was taken prisoner. This led to a royal compromise sanctioned by Parliament: Henry would continue to reign during his lifetime and Richard of York would succeed him, in place of Henry's only son, Edward the infant Prince of Wales. This arrangement naturally enraged Queen Margaret, who vowed to fight for her son's rightful inheritance.

In December 1460 Margaret raised an army and lured Richard, with

After the death of his father, Richard of York, Edward led the Yorkist cause aided by Lord Warwick. In March of 1461 he was proclaimed Edward IV.

jibes at his lack of courage, out of his castle near Wakefield and into an ambush in which he was killed. When Richard's second son, the sixteen-year-old Duke of Rutland, fell to his knees and begged for mercy, Lord Clifford (whose father had fallen at St Albans) stabbed the boy to death, saying, 'As your father killed mine, so I will kill you.' Such was the spirit of this vicious civil war, in which vengeance and retribution replaced chivalry and mercy.

Richard's head was cut off and, wearing a paper crown in mockery, impaled over the gate of York, together with the heads of his son and that of the Earl of Salisbury. It is said that the victorious Margaret jeered, 'Take care to leave room for Warwick's head.' The Yorkist cause was now taken up by Richard's eldest son, Edward, who proved himself a notable general; he was greatly aided by Lord Warwick.

Several battles later, Edward marched triumphantly into London, a city always steady in the Yorkist cause, where he was proclaimed Edward IV of England on 3 March 1461, even though King Henry was still alive. If the feeble Henry could do nothing about the odd situation, Margaret was still full of fight and determined that her son should wear the crown. A few weeks after his proclamation as King, the nineteen year-old Edward IV was facing a Lancastrian army near Towton in Yorkshire.

The battle of Towton, 29 March 1461, one of the most sanguinary conflicts ever fought in England, took place in a snowstorm. Edward's army numbered some 15,000 men and the opposing force, commanded by the young Duke of Somerset, totalled about 20,000 men. Both armies were deployed in the usual formation of the time, three separate divisions, or battles – the vanguard, middleguard, and rearguard – each with its own commander.

The divisions were either placed in three successive lines, or in line abreast, with the vanguard on the right, the middleguard in the centre under the king or the chief commander, and the rearguard on the left. At Towton Edward formed his battles in line abreast, and the Lancastrians were deployed in like manner. Edward was mounted on a horse trapped in crimson velvet adorned with radiant suns and white roses, the badges of his family. On his helmet was the lion of England. As the opposing lines drew near, he dismounted to fight on foot.

At nine in the morning, shrewdly using the advantage of a keen wind blowing the falling snow into the faces of the enemy, Edward sent forward a

The battle of Towton, 29 March 1461. The victorious Yorkists are shown here pursuing the shattered Lancastrians across the River Cock. Illustration by R. Caton Woodville.

Death of Warwick the Kingmaker in the battle of Barnet,
14 April 1471.

skirmish line of archers to execute a stratagem. The archers let fly a single
volley, then retired some distance. The Lancastrian bowmen, having
suffered the bite of the enemy arrows and thinking themselves in range,
returned fire, shooting blindly into the blizzard. But owing to the driving
wind and the retirement of the enemy, their arrows fell short.

The Yorkist bowmen advanced again, unloosed another volley and
retired, having retrieved the wasted shafts of the enemy. Finally, after
repeating the stratagem several times, with the result that the Lancastrians
were out of arrows, Edward's archers moved forward and held their ground,
shooting a great barrage of barbs, many of which had originated from the
enemy.

The two sides clashed in close combat. 'A fearful struggle and butchery
ensued; both armies were alike brave, and both were inspired by the most
rancorous hate.' Soon the field was covered with dead and dying and the
thick snow stained with blood. All morning they hacked, jabbed, and
battered each other with sword, poleaxe, pike and mace, with neither side
giving way. In the afternoon the battle turned in favour of the Yorkists
when the Duke of Norfolk arrived with reinforcements and, screened by the
blizzard, plunged into the enemy's left flank, driving them from the field
and leaving the vanguard and middleguard exposed.

The hard-pressed Lancastrians lost heart and broke, fleeing across the River Cock, pursued by the relentless enemy who cut them down in the water. Various estimates of the casualties suffered by both sides range from 18,000 dead and wounded to 28,000 killed. Six high-ranking nobles died in the fight and several were executed afterwards. King Henry and Margaret, who had been waiting in York for news of the battle, fled to Scotland; Margaret later sought refuge in France, Henry was captured and imprisoned in the Tower of London.

Edward IV was crowned in June 1461. Three years later he secretly married a commoner, Dame Elizabeth Grey (of the Woodville family), widow of a slain Lancastrian, a controversial union that led to Warwick deserting the king he had helped put on the throne. Richard Neville, Earl of Warwick was the greatest, richest, most powerful noble in the land. His services to King Edward had been handsomely rewarded by vast estates confiscated from Lancastrians, and by his elevation to the highest posts of the State.

He was Lieutenant of Ireland, Captain-General of Calais, Captain of Dover, Warden of the Western Marches, Lord Chamberlain, and Lord High Steward. His brothers and relations filled other high offices. Warwick could 'raise armies at his call from his own Earldoms. Six hundred liveried retainers followed him to Parliament.' In war he was a general rather than a warrior. His genius was not so much military as political; he excelled in intrigue.

The new queen was quick in obtaining titles and offices for her numerous relations, replacing Warwick's ministers with her own. Soon the court was loud with the quarrels and jealousies and bitter rivalries between the Woodvilles and the Nevilles. This undermining of his power and influence turned Warwick against Edward and he resolved to place the Duke of Clarence, the king's brother, on the throne. He took up arms against Edward and after a few battles, Warwick and Clarence were obliged to flee to France, where the Kingmaker became reconciled with Queen Margaret, married his daughter to the young Prince of Wales, and made plans for a new Lancastrian attempt to grab the throne of England.

Warwick returned and forced Edward to seek refuge in France with his brother-in-law, the Duke of Burgundy. The Kingmaker released Henry VI and swore allegiance to him, knowing full well that he would pull the strings of the royal puppet. Edward raised an army of some 1,500 men, mostly German and Flemish mercenaries, the latter armed with hand-guns, landed

On winning the battle of
Tewkesbury, 4 May 1471,
King Edward had Henry VI's
son, Prince Edward, brought
before him. When the young
prince answered him boldly
Edward knocked him down
and had him killed on the
spot.

in the Humber Estuary and marched south to London. Lancastrian forces moved to meet him. However, there was yet more treachery. The Duke of Clarence defected and rejoined Edward, bringing with him 4,000 men.

Edward clashed with Warwick in the battle of Barnet on 14 April 1471. The Yorkist army numbered some 9,000 men and the Lancastrians about 12,000. The opposing forces faced each other with their divisions formed in line abreast. Warwick commanded the middleguard, with the vanguard under the Earl of Somerset and the rearguard under the Earl of Oxford. On the other side, Edward commanded the centre, his eighteen year-old brother Richard of Gloucester (who later became Richard III) led the battle on the right, and Lord Hastings the left.

Both armies had artillery. Edward, in bringing his troops into position under cover of darkness, had made the error (a fortunate one as it turned out) of placing them closer to the enemy than he had intended, or Warwick suspected. On realizing that Edward was deploying his men, Warwick opened up with his artillery. Edward held his fire, lest he gave away his true position. The Lancastrian guns overshot the close Yorkist lines and the balls fell harmlessly in the rear. Warwick's guns blasted away most of the night to no effect, wasting their ammunition.

The battle proper opened in the early morning, a thick mist covered the field. In taking up his ground in the dark, Edward had mis-aligned his three divisions with those of the enemy; his battle on the right was extended farther than the Lancastrian counterpart, and his battle on the left fell short of the opposite enemy division. Thus Edward's left flank was vulnerable to a turning movement by the enemy, but Warwick's left flank was equally exposed.

Richard of Gloucester immediately seized the opportunity open to him and tried to envelop Warwick's left, while Edward moved against the centre. Meanwhile, the Earl of Oxford, commanding the Lancastrian right-hand battle made positive use of his advantage and succeeded in turning the enemy's left flank, chasing them off the field. Oxford pursued the broken division all the way to Barnet. However, when Oxford marched back to the battlefield an error in recognition worked in Edward's favour.

In the mist, Oxford's banner of the five-pointed star was mistaken by the Lancastrians for that of Edward's radiant sun, and Oxford's troops were fired on and attacked by their own side. Shouts of 'Treachery!' rose from Oxford's ranks and the rumour spread that Warwick's brother, Montague, had gone over to Edward. Suddenly, all was confusion in the Lancastrian army and they began to scatter. Seeing the enemy in disarray, Edward pressed his advantage and the Lancastrians broke on all sides. Warwick himself, dismounted, made off to find his horse in order to escape, but was caught by pursuers and killed on the spot. When the slaughter ceased, 1,500 bodies littered the field.

On the day of Warwick's defeat and death, Queen Margaret and Prince Edward (now eighteen) landed at Weymouth and in short time had raised an army, including the remnants of Warwick's force at Barnet. Edward brought Margaret's army to battle a few miles from Tewkesbury on 4 May 1471. The two forces faced each other in the usual formation, three battles in a single line, the Yorkists with the largest number of men. King Edward, suspecting an attack from a wood on his left flank, posted 200 spearmen to counter it.

Margaret withdrew to Tewkesbury, leaving Prince Edward in titular command of her army, supported by the Duke of Somerset, Lord Wenlock, and the Earl of Devon. King Edward opened the fight with a bombardment of gun-shots and arrows. Somerset replied by advancing his vanguard on the right in an attack on Edward's middleguard. The move was screened by trees and a hillock and it took the king by surprise.

Somerset had expected direct support from the Lancastrian centre division, commanded by Wenlock and the prince, but the division did not move. Somerset saw treachery (Wenlock was a proven turncoat). At this critical moment Richard of Gloucester, on the king's left, led his battle to attack Somerset, the 200 spearmen also added their weight. Somerset's division was cut to pieces. The duke escaped back to his own lines, there he sought out Wenlock, denounced him a traitor and bashed his brains out with an axe.

The Yorkists advanced and the disheartened enemy fell apart. Somerset and the Earl of Devon were killed, so too was Prince Edward, whose inexperience in battle had contributed to his defeat. There is a story that the prince was captured and taken before King Edward on the field, who asked, 'What brought you here?' To which the prince replied, 'I came to recover my father's kingdom.' Angered by the boy's boldness, Edward struck him in the face with his armoured fist and had him killed on the spot. Most of the other captured Lancastrian nobles were also slaughtered.

Margaret was taken but her life was spared; a broken woman now that her beloved son was dead, she remained in captivity for five years until ransomed by the King of France. She was finished with the Wars of the Roses. On King Edward's return to London on 21 May 1471, poor King

Henry met with a mysterious death in the Tower, some say he was killed by Richard of Gloucester, that rising son of York.

The double-dealing Duke of Clarence and Gloucester squabbled over the great estates of the dead Warwick. Intrigue, discontent, and hatred landed Clarence in the Tower, where he too met a mysterious end in 1478, leaving his brother Gloucester in a very strong position. On the death of Edward IV in 1483 he was succeeded by his eldest son, Edward, a lad of twelve. But the boy king was never crowned; his reign lasted two months. Taken under the protection of the ambitious Gloucester, Edward and his young brother, Richard, Duke of York, were lodged in the Tower and there put to death. Now no one stood between Richard and the crown. His coronation as Richard III took place on 6 July 1483.

He sat on an uneasy throne for he had many enemies. In October the Duke of Buckingham rose in revolt; he and other nobles conspired to place Henry Tudor, Earl of Richmond, on the throne of England. Tudor, head of the House of Lancaster, was living in exile in France; his claim to the crown was a slender one, but thereagain he was the only suitable candidate. It was also planned that Henry should marry Princess Elizabeth of York, daughter of Edward IV, thus uniting the two rival houses (or more romantically, joining the red rose with the white).

Richard III, wearing his crown, at the battle of Bosworth, 22 August 1485, last battle of the Wars of the Roses.

King Richard crushed Buckingham's rising and executed the duke. Henry Tudor was undeterred and early in August 1485 landed at Milford Haven, in Wales, with 3,000 French mercenaries, 'the worst that could be found in Normandy'. He marched inland under the Red Dragon banner, his claim of descent from Cadwaladr bringing Welshmen to his army. He met Richard in battle on marshy ground near the town of Market Bosworth, Leicestershire, on 22 August 1485. Tudor now had an army some 5,000 strong to oppose Richard's 12,000 men.

The king had the advantage in military terms. His army was larger and of better quality than the enemy. Richard was a veteran and skilled field commander; Tudor had little or no battle experience. Richard should have won the day, but treachery decided the battle against him. His chief concern before the fight was the wavering loyalty of Lord Stanley and his brother Sir William, who commanded two separate forces totalling 8,000 men. Ostensibly in Richard's service, the brothers had secretly assured Henry Tudor of their support, but he could not be sure of them until they revealed their true colours on the field of battle.

As the armies of Henry and Richard faced each other, the two Stanleys with their forces stood off at a distance, to the north and south, waiting to see how the battle went before committing themselves. Their intervention would be vital to the outcome.

Richard, mounted on a white horse and wearing full armour, a gold crown on his helmet, commanded the middleguard; the faithful Duke of Norfolk led the battle on the right, the dubious Earl of Northumberland that on the left. In both armies the order of battle was nearly the same: the archers and cannons in front, the billmen in the rear, the horsemen on the wings. Having exchanged cannon fire and arrows, Richard ordered the advance and the two sides closed in the shock of combat, clanging and banging with sword, axe, and mace.

Richard had advanced with his middleguard and vanguard, but Northumberland refused to commit his division in the attack. He held back waiting to see what the enigmatic Stanleys would do. And the Stanleys, observing Northumberland's inactivity, decided now was the time to join Henry Tudor and they struck Richard's loyal troops on both flanks.

Shouting 'Treason! Treason!' Richard, mad with anger, spurred his horse towards the Red Dragon banner of Tudor, hoping to snatch victory from defeat by killing his rival in single combat. Here is the account from *Grafton's Chronicle* of the sixteenth century:

'The Earl of Richmond [Henry Tudor] perceived well the king furiously coming towards him, and because the whole hope of his wealth and purpose was to be determined by battle, he gladly proffered to encounter with him body to body, man to man [in actual fact Henry would have stood little chance against Richard in single combat]. King Richard set on so sharply at the first brunt, that he overthrew and slew Sir William Brandon, the earl's standard bearer, and matched hand to hand with Sir John Cheiney, a man of great force and strength, who would have resisted him, but the said Sir John was by him [Richard] manfully overthrown, and, so making open passage by dent of sword as he went forward. The Earl of Richmond withstood his violence, and kept him at the sword's point without advantage longer than his companions either thought or judged, who, being in almost despair of victory, were suddenly recomforted by Sir William Stanley who came in succour with three thousand tall men, at which very instant King Richard's men were driven back and fled, and he himself manfully fighting in the middle of his enemies was slain.'

Lord Stanley, the grand opportunist, picked up Richard's fallen crown and placed it upon Henry Tudor's head, and the soldiers loudly acclaimed him king. The triumphant Henry rode into Leicester followed by the naked body of Richard, covered in dirt and gore, slung over a horse, 'like a hog or a calf, his head and arms hanging on the one side of the horse, and the legs on the other side'. Six months later Tudor, as Henry VII, married Elizabeth of York and brought the Wars of the Roses to an end.

Chapter Twelve   THE ITALIAN WARS

T HE MIDDLE AGES came to an end with the close of the fifteenth century. Feudalism, based on the bond of land for military service, was being superseded by a money-based economy. Plague had drastically reduced the population of Europe; the subsequent shortage of labour brought about a general change from payment in kind to payment in money.

In war a new professionalism prevailed. This was the golden age of the mercenary. The increased technology of firearms and artillery transformed the art of war to a science. However, strong medieval elements persisted, in particular the use of heavily armoured cavalry. This transitional military mixture is best illustrated in the Italian Wars of the first half of the sixteenth century.

The Lombard invasions and the rise of the Papal States broke up the unity of Italy in the early Middle Ages. City States, such as Venice, Florence, Milan, Naples and Genoa rose to great power in the fragmented country. Civil wars and foreign intervention made Italy a battleground of bloody rivalry. Italy, heart of the Renaissance, was a grand prize for any conqueror; her cities were spectacularly wealthy from the exploits of her merchant-

The Italian Wars of the first
half of the 16th century fused
the dying elements of
medieval warfare with a new
technology of firearms and
artillery.

adventurers and the skills of her craftsmen and artists.

In 1494 Charles VIII of France invaded Italy and began a series of wars that were to establish the Valois and Hapsburg dynasties as the two superpowers of Renaissance Europe. The City States, weakened and divided by their own conflicts, could offer little resistance to the intruders, and changed sides as the occasion suited them.

Charles invaded Italy to capture Naples as the initial step towards a Crusade against the Moslems, a Crusade that never materialized. His action immediately aroused Spain, for Naples was an Aragonese dominion. With continuous fighting and a succession of monarchs the conflict developed until Italy was the principal battleground for the European power struggle.

From 1521 until the end of the wars in 1559 the fighting was dominated by the personal rivalry between Francis I the Valois King of France and Charles V, Holy Roman Emperor of Spain, Naples, Burgundy and the Hapsburg lands of Germany.

Charles VIII's invasion force embodied the new approach to warfare. His army consisted of three equal military parts: cavalry, infantry, and a large artillery train – the basis of all armies for centuries to come. His force of 25,000 men included 8,000 Swiss mercenaries, the finest soldiers that could be hired. They were hard fighters and hard businessmen, their motto being 'pas d'argent, pas de Suisses' ('no money, no Swiss').

If there was a hint of no payment, the Swiss would think nothing of refusing to fight or even of changing sides on the eve of battle. They could afford to act in this capricious manner having established the reputation of being the best soldiers in Europe. Their tactics had been forged in their fight

‡177‡

The Italian Wars saw the final
fling of the mounted knight
in his full panoply of glory.
Pictured here, the battle of
Fornovo, 1495.

for independence against the Hapsburg Knighthood and remained just as effectively simple a century later.

The main body of their force consisted of three densely-packed phalanxes in which the principal weapons were the twenty-one-foot pike and the eight-foot halberd. Highly disciplined and possessed of great courage, they would advance at intimidating speed against any enemy regardless of numbers and composition. In the battle of St Jakob in 1444 Swiss *élan* and determination to neither give nor accept quarter was superbly demonstrated when 1,000 of them attacked a French army thirty times larger. Rather than retreat, the Swiss were annihilated but at the cost of twice as many dead French cavalry and infantry.

Because of their many successes and fierce charisma the Swiss had a psychological advantage over their opponents; it was said that enemy armies 'were half beaten before a blow was struck'. However, despite the great revolution in medieval warfare the Swiss were slow to adopt firearms and refused to use artillery. Subsequently, as the Italian Wars progressed the Swiss found their tactics stereotyped and vulnerable in the face of massed firearms and cannon bombardment.

Following the Swiss pattern, the Germans produced a rival force which used exactly the same tactics. These '*Landsknechts*' (land- or lance-knights) originally included German nobility among their ranks, but as they became much in demand as mercenaries they were joined by men of all types from all over Europe. Soon the Landsknechts gained a notoriety equal to that of

The German Landsknecht pikemen were modelled on the Swiss and gained an equal reputation for ferocity.

‡179‡

Gaston de Foix, a French noble, was an outstanding commander of the Italian Wars whose daring exploits won him the cognomen 'Thunderbolt of Italy'.

the Swiss: it was said of a dead Landsknecht who had been barred from heaven that his conduct so frightened the devil that he was refused entry into hell. Whenever the Landsknechts and the Swiss clashed in battle the conflict was always intense and ruthless with no prisoners taken; the Swiss, however, always seemed to have the edge.

The 'Condottiere' were mercenaries peculiar to Italy; their name was derived from the Italian condotto, meaning conduct, the conduct referred to being strictly financial. At the conclusion of the Hundred Years War many soldiers were unemployed. Having become accustomed to warfare they could not settle in any other way of life. Large numbers of them made their way to Italy and were organized into efficient mercenary companies by the Condottiere captains, who made fortunes hiring out their companies to the constantly feuding City States of the fifteenth century.

Many Condottiere captains became very powerful; sometimes their payment took the form of land and subsequently they rose to influential positions within the cities they had defended. One such man was Francesco Sforza ('stormer' of cities) who was chosen by the Milanese to command their army and, in 1450, made himself their duke and lord. He then extended his sovereignty over Ancona, Pesaro, all Lombardy and Genoa, leaving his family to rule after him.

The 16th century saw an increase in interest in the science and philosophy of war. The two strange war machines shown here, from *l'Art Militaire,* 1532, remained figments of the imagination.

The Condottiere had acute business sense. They managed to preserve their companies from costly, bloody conflicts by avoiding pitched battles, preferring to engage in long sieges. When two Condottiere armies were forced into open battle the opposing commanders would carry out a series of elaborate manoeuvres until one commander was in such an untenable position that he would admit defeat and surrender. These tactical contests have been described as 'chess matches', 'wargames', and *opéra bouffe*.

Most Condottiere soldiers wore full plate armour, thus further reducing the probability of casualties and giving their conflicts a curiously archaic style. In times of peace or when there were no clients, the companies would degenerate into gangs of bandits and ravage the countryside. The Italians became inured to this danger and as soon as a mercenary force approached they would bury their valuables and retire within the nearest city.

There are many accounts of Condottiere atrocities, of which the following is typical: 'In passing through a certain place they chanced upon a wedding celebration; they cut down the bridegroom and wedding guests, violated the women, looted all the table and silverware, stripped the women of their clothes and carried off the bride.' The local inhabitants retaliated by killing any isolated mercenaries they found. The power of the Condottiere was broken by the superior army of Charles VIII of France.

Another aspect of Renaissance warfare that distinguished it from the

Skin-diver and underwater warrior as predicted in *l'Art Militaire*, 1532.

medieval period was the increased interest in the science and philosophy of
war, a development initiated by the new technology of artillery and firearms as well as by the intensified economics and politics of campaigning. In
1537 Niccolo Tartaglia published the first scientific treatise on ballistics. In
1550 Charles V, the Holy Roman Emperor, standardized all his artillery into
seven types to ease the supply of ammunition.

By the end of the century three main classes of artillery had emerged: the
long range 'culverin', the more powerful short range cannon, and the high
trajectory mortar. In defence against artillery new methods of fortification
were tried and tested until low forts with earth emplacements revived the
arduous tradition of siege warfare from the high Middle Ages.

In other fields of military theory the work of Niccolo Machiavelli was
particularly notable. Being an Italian he despised the prevalence of mercenaries, favouring instead the creation of militia forces. Recalling the classical
Roman army, he suggested that infantry should be armed in similar manner
to the legionaries. This was to a certain extent put into effect by the Spanish
who armed some companies with sword and buckler (a small round shield).
However, Machiavelli underestimated the power of firearms and pre-
maturely dismissed the fortress. Leonardo da Vinci contributed to military
science with designs for pontoons, bombs, mortars, armoured vehicles and
various siege machines.

Francis I of France surrenders
his sword in the chivalric
manner after his defeat at
Pavia in 1525.

‡184‡

The early years of the Italian Wars were dominated by the brilliant Spanish commander Hernandez Gonzalo de Córdoba, who twice reconquered Naples from the French with his flexible tactics. After losing his first major battle at Seminara in 1495, Cordoba concentrated on frequent raiding attacks, probably based on experience from his campaigns against the Moors. He quickly adapted his army to the Swiss military system by training his own pike divisions, and also arming a force in classical style with a short thrusting sword and buckler and protecting them with metal leg greaves, breastplate and steel helmet. The sword and buckler men were to enjoy considerable success in future battles.

Córdoba has been called the 'father of trench warfare' from his penchant of placing soldiers armed with the arquebus (an early type of matchlock firearm) behind earthwork entrenchments. The Spaniards had been quick to adopt the arquebus, whereas the French had not. Córdoba's faith in firearms was proved in the battle of Cerignola in 1503, when the massed fire of the Spanish arquebusiers, protected by ditch and pallisade, swept the Swiss infantry and French cavalry off the field – probably the first battle to be won by firearms.

Córdoba became Viceroy of Naples but by 1507 King Ferdinand of Spain considered him too powerful; he was recalled and spent the rest of his life on his estate at Granada. The next great commander of the Italian Wars was Gaston de Foix, a French noble. At the age of twenty-one he had routed two Swiss armies, driven the Pope from Bologna, seized Brescia from the Venetians, and won the sobriquet 'Thunderbolt of Italy'. The climax of his career came with his victory over the Spanish at Ravenna in 1512.

The battle opened with a heavy artillery barrage from de Foix's fifty-four guns, which pounded the enemy's stout earthwork defence. The Spanish infantry were virtually untouched but the cavalry were less well-positioned and the bombardment provoked the horsemen into a rash, unordered attack which was repulsed. De Foix now counter-attacked, his Landsknechts valiantly assaulted the Spanish entrenchments with many casualties on both sides. In the midst of the fighting de Foix displayed his genius by utilizing the improved mobility of artillery by sending two guns across the river that protected the Spanish rear. The guns caused great havoc and the Spaniards retreated with de Foix's soldiers in pursuit.

A group of Landsknechts ran after a column of fleeing Spaniards, who were armed with the sword and buckler. To the Germans surprise, the enemy suddenly turned round and, as Machiavelli tells us, 'rushed at the

Chevalier de Bayard, a true son of chivalry renowned as the 'knight without fear and without reproach'.

pikes, threw themselves on the ground and slipped below the points, so that they darted in among the legs of the pikemen and made such good use of their swords that not one of the enemy would have been left alive, had not a body of French cavalry come to rescue them'.

Gaston de Foix won the day but was killed in a skirmish at his moment of victory. From his achievements in a short but glorious life it has been said that de Foix would have become one of the greatest captains of all time. From 1515 to 1547 Francis I led France against Charles V in four Valois–Hapsburg wars. A daring warrior from his youth, Francis was captured in the battle of Pavia in 1525 and taken to Madrid, where to gain his freedom he signed a treaty which he later repudiated.

After Francis died and Charles abdicated, the struggle was continued by their successors until 1559 when the Peace of Catteau-Cambresis saw France give up all her land and claims in Italy. The Wars of Religion were now to dominate Europe in the last stages of the Renaissance. The gun was

The heroic Bayard died in battle in 1524, a celebrated knight cut down by a bullet fired by an unknown foot-soldier.

The end of the Middle Ages saw the end of the armoured knight as the principal force in battle. His thousand-year dominance was over. Guns and infantry were now the decisive factors in warfare.

in the ascendancy. The Middle Ages had finally ended. The story of the Chevalier de Bayard makes a fitting conclusion.

Pierre du Terrail, Chevalier de Bayard, was renowned as the 'knight without fear and without reproach', a paladin of the highest quality. Born in 1476 in the Château Bayard, near Grenoble, his family was celebrated for nobility and valour. As a youth he excelled in the tournaments. At eighteen he accompanied Charles VIII to Italy and distinguished himself in the battle of Fornovo, where he took a standard.

In Apulia he defeated a Spanish force and captured its leader, Don Alonzo de Sotomayor, whom he treated with generosity. Sotomayor, however, violated his parole by escape and spoke evilly of Bayard, who challenged the Spaniard and killed him. Afterwards, like Horatius, he defended a bridge over the Garigliano single-handed and saved the French army by checking the enemy advance. He distinguished himself equally against the Genoese and the Venetians.

Being wounded in the assault of Brescia he was carried into the house of a nobleman who had fled, leaving his wife and daughters exposed to the insolence of the soldiers. In the finest spirit of chivalry, Bayard protected the family and refused the reward of 2,500 ducats which they offered him.

After many exploits which won him fame and admiration from his countrymen and enemies alike, Bayard died in battle fighting the Spaniards in Italy on 30 April 1524. A bullet from an arquebus shattered his backbone. Mortally wounded, he asked to be placed with his back against a tree, 'So that I may die as I have lived, with my face to the foe.' For want of a crucifix he kissed the cross of his sword, confessed to his squire, consoled his servants and his friends, and died. Even the Spaniards shed tears of grief.

So passed the great Chevalier de Bayard, the last true knight embued with the chivalric spirit of the Middle Ages – shot in the back by an unknown foot-soldier.

A SELECT BIBLIOGRAPHY

ASHDOWN, C. *Armour and Weapons in the Middle Ages*, London, 1925

BARBER, R. *The Knight and Chivalry*, London, 1970

BRYANT, A. *The Age of Chivalry*, London, 1963

COLE, H. *The Wars of the Roses*, London, 1973

DEMMIN, A. *Arms and Armour*, London, 1901

DUPUY, R. E. and T. N. *Encyclopedia of Military History*, London, 1970

FOWLER, K.(ed.) *The Hundred Years War*, London, 1971

HARDY, R. *Longbow*, Cambridge, 1976

HOWARD, M. *War in European History*, Oxford, 1976

LANDER, J. *Wars of the Roses*, London, 1965

LOYN, H. R. *The Norman Conquest*, London, 1967

MANUCY, A. *Artillery Through the Ages*, Washington, D.C., 1949

MAYER, H. E. *The Crusades*, Oxford, 1972

MONTGOMERY OF ALAMEIN. *History of Warfare*, London, 1968

MORRIS, J. *The Welsh Wars of Edward the First*, Oxford, 1901

NORMAN AND POTTINGER *Warrior to Soldier 449–1660*, London, 1966

NORMAN, V. *The Medieval Soldier*, London, 1971

OAKESHOTT, R. E. *A Knight and his Armour*, Guildford, 1961

OMAN, SIR CHARLES. *A History of the Art of War in the Middle Ages*, London, 1924

TREECE, H. *The Crusades*, London, 1962

WARNER, P. *The Medieval Castle*, London, 1971

WISE, T. *Medieval Warfare*, London, 1976